PROGRAM DEVELOPMENT AND EVALUATION RESOURCE BOOK FOR TRAINERS

WILEY SERIES IN TRAINING AND DEVELOPMENT

Editor:
Charles T. Peers, Jr.

PROGRAM DEVELOPMENT AND EVALUATION RESOURCE BOOK FOR TRAINERS

Rosemary S. Caffarella

Virginia Commonwealth University
Richmond, Virginia

JOHN WILEY & SONS

New York   **Chichester**   **Brisbane**   **Toronto**   **Singapore**

Library of Congress Cataloging-in-Publication Data

Caffarella, Rosemary S. (Rosemary Shelly), 1946-
   Program development and evaluation resource book for trainers.

   (Wiley series in training and development)
   Bibliography: p.
   1. Employees, Training of–Evaluation–Handbooks,
manuals, etc.   2. Employees, Training of–Case studies.
3. Employees, Training of–Problems, exercises, etc.
I. Title. II. Series.
HF5549.5.T7C23 1987   658.3'12404   87–15990
ISBN 0-471-84235-4

Printed in the United States of America

10 9 8 7 6 5 4 3 2 1

To Edward, my husband
and Christy, my daughter.

PREFACE

Developing training programs is like trying to negotiate a maze successfully. Sometimes we manage to get through the maze quickly, and feel a real sense of satisfaction that we could do it with such ease. Other times we constantly run into dead ends and have to retrace our steps, which can be frustrating and yet challenging. So it is with program planning. Some of our programs run smoothly from start to finish, and we feel good about those programs. Others seem to wander all over the place, with lots of revisions and changes in plans. When these programs have successful endings, we feel a real sense of accomplishment and satisfaction with our work. I wrote this book to assist people who must "run this maze" of program planning as part of their daily job responsibilities.

The book constitutes a kind of how-to-do-it manual for program planners and evaluators. It can serve as a practical reference guide and a workbook for building competencies in program development. The readers will find the worksheets at the end of each chapter especially useful in applying the material to their own work situations. This book is intended for people who plan, conduct, and evaluate training programs in all types of organizations, from business and industry to hospitals and voluntary associations.

I would like to acknowledge the special help I have received in preparing this manuscript:

To Nancy Berger, Sylvia Fine, Shelley Johnson, Richard Leatherman, Judy O'Donnell, Rhonda Sadler, and Linda Seeman for their careful critique and editing of the book.

To Rhonda Sadler and Blue Cross and Blue Shield of Virginia for their willingness to test out and use the program development model. I am especially grateful to Rhonda for her assistance in developing Chapter 16.

To Susan Goins, my typist, without whom the book would still be in an illegible form.

To Ed Caffarella, my husband and Christy Caffarella, my daughter for all their support, love, and patience.

ROSEMARY S. CAFFARELLA

Richmond, Virginia
September 1987

CONTENTS

TABLES

WORKSHEETS

WORKSHEETS

FIGURES

1

INTRODUCTION

Planning and evaluating training programs is both an organized and haphazard endeavor. On the surface, it appears to be a fairly logical and orderly process, progressing from needs assessment to program design and implementation to evaluation and follow-up activities. Yet, for those persons who actually develop and coordinate training programs, the process seems to be more a mass of details and deadlines than precise and clear steps of what should be done when, where, how, and by whom. The purpose of this book is to assist personnel responsible for training to become more systematic in their program development activities and, at the same time, help them to recognize that their tasks can never be totally organized or at times even remotely logical or orderly. Rather, program planning and evaluation is a dynamic process, set within the confines of ever changing organizational needs, priorities, and values.

WHO IS THIS BOOK FOR?

The intended audience for this book are persons responsible for planning and evaluating training programs in all types of organizations, from business and industry to hospitals and voluntary associations. The book can serve as a practical guide for full-time training specialists and for persons who are required to plan and conduct training activities as only a small portion of their work activities. It will be useful for personnel involved with:

Technical training

Supervisory and management development

Sales and marketing training

New employee orientation

Staff development

Volunteer training

HOW IS THE BOOK ORGANIZED?

The book is organized into three major areas. The first area lays the groundwork by introducing what program planning is all about and the model of the program planning and evaluation to be used as the basis for the rest of the book. More specifically, Chapter 2 describes the whys, whats, hows, and whos of the program planning function and should be especially useful to novice trainers and people who think they may be in the training business but are not sure. Chapter 3 can assist the reader in gaining a better understanding of how using a program planning model can actually help them plan more effective training activities, with more ease and less hassle. Chapter 4 presents an overview of a practical and workable model of program development and evaluation, to be discussed in detail in Chapters 5 through 15. The model can serve as a map or series of checkpoints to help training personnel move through the maze of people, places, and paperwork involved in planning and conducting training activities.

The second area of the book constitutes a kind of how-to-do-it manual for program planners and evaluators. Each component of the program planning and evaluation model is explained in-depth as follows:

Identifying the Basis for Program Development (Chapter 5)

Compiling and Analyzing Training Needs (Chapter 6)

Determining Priorities for Training (Chapter 7)

Identifying Program Objectives (Chapter 8)

Determining Potential Trainees, The Program Format, and Staff (Chapter 9)

Coordinating Program Arrangements and Logistics (Chapter 10)

Preparing Instructional Plans (Chapter 11)

Formulating a Continuous Evaluation Component (Chapter 12)

Carrying Out the Program (Chapter 13)

Measuring and Appraising the Results of the Program (Chapter 14)

Communicating the Value of the Program to the Appropriate Publics (Chapter 15)

Case scenarios and practical examples are given to demonstrate how each component can be applied in the work setting.

The final chapter is a case study of how the model was applied to an actual program development situation within a large health-related organization. The case chronicles how the model was used over a four-month period to develop a major training program for internal staff and external provider organizations.

HOW TO USE THE BOOK

There are several ways this book can be used depending on the reader's own interests and needs. It can serve as a practical reference guide for persons interested in the overall program planning and evaluation process. This might include novice training personnel who just want to get a feel for what their jobs are all about, to more experienced trainers, and training managers who wish to compare this model with others in the field and possibly adapt parts or all of the process into their own work.

Another way to use the book is to have persons responsible for training keep it on their bookshelf and utilize it as a resource to help them in responding to specific tasks or problems they encounter on the job. For example, Chapter 6, "Compiling and Analyzing Training Needs" might become more interesting and definitely more relevant to staff members—especially ones who know very little about needs assessment—who are asked to assist in putting together a major needs analysis for their organizations.

Training personnel can also use this book to test their knowledge and ability to use the material by completing the worksheets found at the end of most chapters. These worksheets can assist training staff in two ways: (1) in applying the content to their own work as program planners and evaluators, and (2) in enhancing their own skills and competencies to carry out effectively the process of program development and evaluation.

2

THE PROGRAM PLANNING ENTERPRISE

The purpose of this chapter is to introduce the reader to the role and function of persons who plan and conduct training programs within a variety of organizations. This chapter addresses the basic whys, whats, hows, and whos of the program planning enterprise. It will also assist those involved in planning training activities to better understand the process as a whole and their role in that process.

Training programs come in a variety of sizes, shapes, and formats. They vary from month-long seminars at a corporate training center to morning in-house workshops. Programs may be individualized or involve learning in small or large group settings. For example, Bank X may conduct all of its teller training through computer-assisted instruction, whereas Bank Z prefers to train new tellers through small group instruction. A program may be for a small select group of individuals, such as corporate executives, or it may be designed for a large number of people with diverse backgrounds, such as those attending a major national conference or convention for human resource development specialists.

WHY TRAINING IS DONE

Training programs are conducted for three primary purposes: (1) to prepare people to do their jobs (Laird, 1985), (2) to improve present job performance (Nadler, 1985), and (3) to assist departments and whole

TABLE 2.1. Primary Purposes of Training Programs with Examples Given for Each Purpose

Purpose Training Programs	Program Examples
Prepare people to do their jobs	1. Entry-level management training program 2. New worker orientation program 3. Formal apprenticeship training program
Improve present job performance	1. Workshop on stress management for management-level personnel 2. Communication skills workshop for secretaries and receptionists 3. A skills update on the new components of the packaging machine
Assist departments and whole organizations to grow	1. A weekend conference retreat for all mid-level managers in Division A 2. A one-day workshop on improving effectiveness and efficiency for all grade 6 secretarial personnel 3. A quality circles program for all line supervisors

organizations to grow and develop (Laird, 1985; Nadler, 1985). Another purpose of some programs may be to foster the growth and development of the individual, regardless of any direct benefit to the organization. Examples of specific types of training programs illustrating each purpose are outlined in Table 2.1.

WHAT ARE THE PRIMARY OUTCOMES OF TRAINING?

Training programs foster three primary learning outcomes: acquisition of new knowledge, skill building, and attitude change (Laird, 1985; Nadler, 1982; Robinson, 1979). It is important for program planners to have a clear picture of the proposed learning outcomes of a program. All aspects of the design, from the chosen format to the instructors and techniques to be used, depend on the focus (knowledge, skill, attitude change) of these learning outcomes. Specific examples of primary learning outcomes in each of the three learning domains are given in Table 2.2.

TABLE 2.2. Examples of the Primary Learning Outcomes of Training Programs

	Learning Outcomes		
Purpose of the Training Program	Knowledge Acquisition	Skill Building	Attitude Change
Prepare people to do their jobs	Management trainee will be able to describe the seven primary functions of management	Management trainee will be able to prepare a workable budget for a six-month period	Management trainee will display the qualities and behavior of a good "team player"
Improve present job performance	Manager will be able to define the terms conflict and conflict management	Manager will be able to demonstrate at least two alternative ways for handling a specific conflict situation	Manager will demonstrate through both behavior and specific actions that he or she is not afraid of handling a conflict situation
Assist departments and whole organizations	All of the supervisors in Division A will be able to define and describe the process of conducting quality circles	All of the supervisors in Division A will be able to effectively lead a quality circle	All of the supervisors in Division A will display through their behavior a belief in the use of quality circles as one way to improve performance

HOW TRAINING PROGRAMS ARE PLANNED

Some training programs are carefully planned, while others are literally just thrown together. The following scenarios illustrate this point.

SCENARIO ONE. George S. has been asked to coordinate a half-day workshop for all of the technical trainers on teaching techniques. Somehow the date slips his mind and a week before the workshop he realizes he has no instructor for the workshop. He calls the local university hoping he can get the assistance of one of the human resource development professors for the morning. He is in luck, or so he thinks. Professor Bland gives a three-hour lecture on how to teach. Not only is the material old hat to most of the trainers, but the professor, well-versed in management development programs, primarily uses examples from that arena to illustrate his points. The workshop receives consistently low marks from all the participants.

SCENARIO TWO. Bill J. is in charge of developing a half-day workshop for all of his first-line supervisors on "coaching skills." He calls together five of the key supervisors to ask them what they think the supervisors need to learn about this area. Based on the information he gleans from the supervisors, and some discrete observations of supervisory staff, he determines that a one-hour overview and demonstration of basic coaching skills is needed, followed by a two-hour practice session. He asks three supervisors from another division, who are known for their ability to coach their employees, to assist him in putting on the workshop. He also makes sure that a good lunch is served, on the company, at the end of the morning. The workshop is well-received by all participants.

Careful planning of training programs does not guarantee that the programs will be successful, but it does increase the probability for success. It also gives planners better data on which to evaluate their successes and failures.

WHAT DO PROGRAM PLANNERS DO?

What is the "work" of program planners? What types of daily activities constitute either part or all of their day's work? Basically, they perform 14 major tasks in developing and conducting training programs (Caffarella, 1985; Houle, 1972; Knowles, 1980; Laird, 1985; Nadler, 1985; Sork and Buskey, 1986). These 14 work activities are:

1. Identifies and prioritizes needs and ideas for training programs
2. Develops objectives for programs
3. Decides on appropriate program formats
4. Determines potential trainees and staff
5. Selects specific program content
6. Obtains and/or develops instructional plans and resources
7. Selects and obtains instructors and/or serves as instructor
8. Formulates the evaluation component
9. Develops and manages the budget for training programs
10. Arranges training facilities, including housing and meals
11. Prepares program publicity
12. Coordinates the program
13. Evaluates the training program
14. Communicates the results of the program

WHO PLANS TRAINING PROGRAMS?

Not all people doing program planning will be involved in all these activities. Some personnel will only be responsible for one or two of the activities, such as selecting program content or choosing instructors and resources. Others, usually training specialists, will be involved in most or all the activities.

WHO PLANS TRAINING PROGRAMS?

Training programs are planned and coordinated by a number of different types of personnel (Gane, 1972). Only a minority of people responsible for training programs have the title of training specialist or some equivalent. Let us consider three different employees in diverse organizations. Though each person is responsible for planning training programs, the breadth and centrality of that responsibility is quite different for each.

Program Planning as a Primary Function

ROBERT B.: INSTRUCTIONAL DEVELOPER. Robert B. is employed as an Instructional Developer for the Blackwell Corporation. He is located at the Corporate Training Center and reports to the Associate Vice President for Human Resource Development. He is one of three instructional developers employed at the corporate level. His major responsibility is to design educational programs for both staff and customers of the company. These programs range from one-hour modules to three-week intensive seminars. Though at times he may actually serve as the instructor for one of the programs, his major job is to develop the program.

In essence, Robert B.'s major role is that of program developer. He functions as a program design specialist (Kemp, 1977; Laird, 1985; Munson, 1984; Nadler, 1985) and is responsible for writing, producing, and evaluating training programs requested by the various divisions within the company. He rarely works alone. Instead, he works in tandem with content specialists, usually company personnel from the division that has requested the program, and/or outside consultants. In addition, he may work with the training center's production group on the development of the instructional materials to be used in the program, or with the center's conference coordinator if the program is to be housed at the center itself.

Program Planning as One
of Multiple Primary Functions

BETTY W.: MANAGER OF TRAINING AND DEVELOPMENT. Betty W. serves as the Manager of Training and Development for the Federal Reserve Bank. She is located in a regional office and reports to the Director of Personnel. Betty has a staff of five people, four trainers and one secretary. In reviewing her calendar for the next day, Betty has made the following notations:

9 A.M. Staff meeting (note: review the training calendar for the next six months)

10:30 A.M. Joe C. (note: lay out the final plans for the agency-wide needs analysis of management-level personnel)

Noon Lunch with Susan M. (her boss) (note: stress the importance of the upcoming management training conference)

2:00 P.M. Sally R. (supervisor in front-desk operations) (note: she wants some assistance with problems of absenteeism and staff morale)

3-5:00 P.M. Conduct workshop on stress management (note: make sure all handouts are ready)

In this one day, Betty W. has assumed four different roles, that of training manager, program developer, consultant, and instructor (Laird, 1985; Munson, 1984; Nadler, 1985). If you were to examine her calendar on successive days, how much time she devotes to each role would change depending on her own plan of work. Thus, although Betty is involved in program development, it is only one of many primary roles that she assumes.

Betty's function as a program planner will vary from actually designing full programs, to serving as a consultant on program planning to line managers and her own staff. She may take charge of parts of the program planning process when she believes this is important or her expertise is especially relevant. For example, Betty may direct an organizational wide needs analysis if she believes obtaining accurate data is crucial to the success of her operation. At other times, she will choose to be involved only in a peripheral way as a program coordinator or informal sounding board for program ideas.

Program Planning as a Secondary Function

JOHN S.: DIRECTOR OF NURSING. John S. is the Director of Nursing of a medium-sized metropolitan hospital. John has a nursing staff of 300, including both full- and part-time employees. He reports directly to the Associate Executive Director of the hospital. He has learned that within a two-month period, a new patient charting system will be installed in the hospital. His job is to ensure that all his nursing staff will be able to use the new charting system in an effective and efficient manner. He has called a meeting of selected head nurses to assist him in responding to this task: how can he get all the nurses trained to use this new system in such a short period of time? Meanwhile, he is having major problems in other areas, including the recruitment of new staff, the settlement of a two-year labor contract, and the resignation of one of his best head nurses.

John S. is also involved in program planning for staff training, but only as a minor part of his job responsibilities. He knows the task has to be done and that it is clearly a part of his job description, but it is a task that both he and his supervisor have relegated to a fairly low priority item. Most of what John S. has chosen to do in this area is to send his staff to programs run by other departments in the hospital or by other organizations. He has invited a few university people to give "clinical updates," but he has delegated all the work on those activities to two of his head nurses. He knows he has to pull this latest training effort off himself, as the executive director of the hospital has made it a priority item.

SUMMARY

1. Training programs are conducted for three primary purposes: (1) to prepare people to do their jobs, (2) to improve present job performance, and (3) to help departments and whole organizations to grow.
2. Training programs foster three kinds of learning outcomes: acquisition of new knowledge, skill development, and attitude change. All aspects of the program design, from the format to the instructors and techniques used, depend on the focus of these learning outcomes.
3. Some training programs are carefully planned; others are literally just thrown together. Although careful planning of training programs does not guarantee those programs will be successful, it does increase the probability for success.

4. Staff perform 14 major tasks in developing and conducting training programs:
   a. Identify and prioritize needs and ideas for training programs
   b. Develop objectives of programs
   c. Decide appropriate program formats
   d. Determine potential trainees and staff
   e. Select specific program content
   f. Obtain and/or develop instructional plans and resources
   g. Select and obtain instructors and/or serve as instructor
   h. Formulate the evaluation component
   i. Develop and manage the budget for training programs
   j. Arrange training facilities, including housing and meals
   k. Prepare program publicity
   l. Coordinate the program
   m. Evaluate the training program
   n. Communicate the results of the program
5. Only a minority of the staff responsible for planning and conducting training programs in organizations have the title of training specialist or some equivalent. Training is often only a part of an individual's other major job responsibilities.

►CHAPTER 2, WORKSHEET 1:
YOUR ROLE AS A PROGRAM PLANNER

1. a. List your present title and give a brief job description.

_____

_____

_____

_____

   b. Is the role of program planner a formal part of your job description? _____ Yes _____ No

2. Check the types of training programs in which you have been involved in the actual planning of that program.

_____ Apprenticeship	_____ Workshop
_____ Coaching	_____ Trip tour
_____ Programmed instruction	_____ Conference
_____ Computer-assisted instruction	_____ Institute
_____ Independent study/reading	_____ Convention
_____ Courses	_____ Lecture series
_____ Seminars	_____ Exhibits

_____ Other (Please Specify) _____

_____

(continued)

3. What types of activities do you get involved with as a program planner and how extensive is that involvement on a day-to-day basis? Please check the appropriate box for each line.

Activities	Not a Part of My Work	Sometimes Is Part of My Work	A Major Part of My Work
Identify and prioritize needs and ideas for training programs			
Develop objectives for programs			
Decide on appropriate program formats			
Determine potential trainees and staff			
Select specific program content			
Obtain and/or develop instructional plans and resources			
Select and obtain instructors and/or serve as instructor			
Formulate the evaluation component			
Develop and manage budgets for programs			

Activities	Not a Part of My Work	Sometimes Is Part of My Work	A Major Part of My Work
Arrange training facilities, including housing and meals			
Prepare program publicity			
Coordinate the programs			
Evaluate the training program			
Communicate the results of the program to others			

1. Outline, on the following chart, the personnel in your organization or a specific subunit of your organization who are responsible for planning and conducting training programs. Indicate whether this responsibility is a formal part of their job description. Then outline, using the list as a guide, the tasks each person does as part of this work.

Tasks Required to Plan and Conduct Training Programs

A. Identify and prioritize needs and ideas for training

B. Develop objectives for programs

C. Decide on appropriate program formats

D. Determine potential trainees and staff

E. Select specific program content

F. Obtain or develop instructional plans and resources

G. Select and obtain instructors

H. Serve as instructor

I. Formulate evaluation component

J. Develop and manage budget

K. Arrange facilities

L. Prepare program publicity

M. Coordinate programs

N. Evaluate the training

O. Communicate the results of the program

Position Name	Part of Formal Job Description Yes or No	Tasks Each Person Does Related to Planning and Conducting Training Programs
1.		
2.		
3.		
4.		
5.		
6.		

2. How might those responsible for program planning be supportive of each other in their efforts? List specific suggestions below.

_____

_____

_____

3

USE OF PROGRAM PLANNING MODELS

Carol C. is completing the final program outline for the upcoming Management Institute on Strategic Planning. She knows she must have a camera-ready copy to the printers by tomorrow to meet the publicity deadline. She realizes she still needs to contact the president's office to see if he can do the opening welcome and get in touch with one of the consultants to confirm her commitment. She is a little uneasy about the presentation proposed by a second consultant: the outline he sent seemed rather vague. She has thought about calling him, but just has not found the time. Carol thinks to herself: is there anything else that I have forgotten at this point? Where is that checklist I developed for myself?

Carol C. is not unusual in the day-to-day reality of planning training programs. Many training personnel become so caught up in the day-to-day operations that it is easy to lose sight of all that needs to be done to plan a successful program. What is helpful to many planners is to have a guide or road map to assist them in getting from the start to the finish of any program.

A model of program planning can provide this needed map or guide. "Models are not in themselves a reality, but they represent the reality of those who have developed them" (Nadler, 1982). Program planning models consist of ideas of one or more persons about how programs should be put together and what ingredients are necessary to ensure a successful outcome.

CHARACTERISTICS OF MODELS OF PROGRAM PLANNING

Models of program planning come in all shapes and sizes. They may be simplistic in their orientation with steps one through five, or very complex, with highly developed flowcharts depicting a comprehensive array of decision points (Kaufman and Stone 1983; Nadler, 1982).

A program planning model is usually conceived as an open or closed system (Nadler, 1982). In a closed system, all inputs to the system can be identified and the outcomes can be both predetermined and ensured. An open system recognizes that outside factors do exist, that these factors can have an impact on the program planning process, and that many of these factors are beyond the control of the planner. Very few training programs can be built based on a closed model system. Simple things like snowstorms and late airplanes and more complex happenings, such as an unplanned but severe budget reduction, can affect both the substance and outcomes of planned programs.

Some models of program planning are presented as linear. For example, if a 10-step model is outlined, the trainer would be expected to start at step one and follow each step in sequential order until the process is completed. This type of model may be helpful to new trainers, but soon loses its appeal because it does not represent the day-to-day working reality of most program planners. An alternative to the linear approach is to conceptualize the program planning process as a set of interacting and dynamic elements or components (Caffarella, 1985; Houle, 1972). This type of model allows the program planner to address a number of the components simultaneously or to rearrange the components to suit the demands of different planning situations.

WHY PROGRAM PLANNING MODELS ARE USEFUL

Building on the work of Munson (1984), five reasons why program planning models can be useful are:

1. Resources are used more effectively
2. Daily work is made easier
3. Teamwork is fostered
4. Basis for management control is provided
5. Better programs are developed

Let us examine each of these reasons more closely for further clarification.

Resources Used More Effectively

Program planning models can assist people to better use their planning resources of people, time, and money. For example, especially for inexperienced program developers, a model can help clarify what they need to do to get a program up and running. Thus time can be saved by not having to figure out all the essential ingredients by themselves and also by not having to go back and do or redo steps they forgot.

Daily Work Is Made Easier

The daily work of program planners can be made easier because a model can provide a continuing guide for action. It is much simpler to plan a program when most of the essential tasks to be done are laid out beforehand.

For example, as shown in Table 3.1, a training manager could, based on a comprehensive model of program development, prepare a checklist of tasks to be accomplished, including a column to write in deadline dates and the person responsible for getting the task accomplished. This could then be used by all persons responsible for developing training programs in the organization as a practical guide for planning programs.

TABLE 3.1. Sample Program Checklist Form

Task to Be Accomplished	Person(s) Responsible	Timetable	
		Immediate Deadline	Final Deadline
Conduct a needs assessment of the potential trainers and their supervisors	Sally Q., Training Specialist	Survey developed 6/1/86 Survey sent out 7/1/86 Survey analyzed 8/1/86	Completed report 9/15/86
Prepare the specific program objectives	Bob R., Training Specialist	Draft 10/1/86	Final 10/15/86
Prepare a budget plan	Susan M., Training Manager		10/1/86
Identify needed staff and resources	Bob R., Training specialist		11/1/86

Teamwork Is Fostered

Teamwork among people responsible for planning a program can also be fostered by using a specific program planning model. A model can provide a means for clarifying roles and responsibilities for all involved, which can lead to a better spirit of team cooperation versus fighting over "who was supposed to do what." Two scenarios illustrate this idea. The scenarios describe a mid-year planning meeting of a local chapter of the American Society for Training and Development (ASTD). The chair has asked each person to review their assignments for the upcoming conference to be hosted by the chapter in a month's time.

SCENARIO ONE. Bill responds to the chair's request by asking if the chair can review again what each of the committee members are to do. He does not remember the specifics, nor does a colleague of his who was not able to attend the meeting. The chair fumbles through his notes of the last meeting trying to figure out just what they said. Meanwhile, two of the members fume because they have completed their responsibilities and were ready to report on them.

SCENARIO TWO. Each person at the session in turn describes what he or she has accomplished. The chair then gives a report for the two missing members. The group as a whole then reviews the next set of tasks as described on the program checklist they had developed three months earlier. Due to some last-minute changes, some minor modifications need to be made to their plan of work, but all agree they are right on target in their development of the conference. They agree to meet in three weeks' time to ensure that all the final arrangements are completed.

Basis for Management Control Is Provided

Using a program planning model can benefit not only the planner, but his or her supervisor. Having a detailed and clear planning procedure can provide a basis for control over both the process and the subordinate's role in that process. This gives a manager an opportunity to coach his or her staff in areas in which they appear weak and to reward them for those tasks they complete effectively and efficiently.

Better Programs Are Developed

An overall better program is usually the result of using a model of program planning. Most models dictate that a closer look be given up front to the problems or needs presented. This helps the planner move beyond just reacting to day-to-day requests for training and crisis situations to being able to analyze carefully those requests and problems and make informed choices about possible courses of action. For example, a manager may request that the training department conduct a seminar on time management for his or her employees. In investigating the request further, the training specialist determines that the problem is not poor management of time by employees, but a severe overload of work. Thus training in time management would not have solved what the manager had originally perceived as the problem unless other changes were made in how the division functioned.

In addition, using a program planning model helps prevent staff members from forgetting to address essential tasks of the program planning process. When these tasks are not done, it leaves holes in the planning process itself and in the final product of that process. For example, the checking of facilities and equipment for an upcoming program is of prime importance. This can lead to disastrous results if not done as illustrated in the following scenario.

SCENARIO THREE. Warren P. has the responsibility for making all final arrangements for a staff development conference. Although he has seen diagrams of the rooms to be used, he did not have the chance, nor did he really see the need, to visit the facilities himself. The hotel staff had assured him that the room space would be adequate and they had an excellent sound system for the main banquet room. When he arrived on the morning of the conference, Warren discovered to his horror, that not only was the sound system inadequate, but a major remodeling project was underway in areas they would be using.

Using a program planning model also alerts staff to the need for sound evaluation procedures. This ensures that the planners know if the program actually produces the results that were proposed, and also provides data for improving future program offerings.

WHY PROGRAM PLANNING MODELS ARE NOT USED

There are four major reasons why staff involved in training do not use a model in the planning of training programs. The first two are drawn from the work of Munson (1984):

1. Time pressures
2. Organizational environment
3. Lack of knowledge about available models
4. Rejection of models as too confining to be helpful

Each of these reasons will be explored in greater detail in the following sections.

Time Pressure

> Sharon's week has been one meeting after the next. She has been working on the strategic plan for the organization, and it is due in two weeks. She also has conducted two half-day training seminars and managed to fit in a workshop for herself conducted by the local American Society for Training and Development (ASTD) chapter. She has three requests sitting on her desk for future training programs, which she has not had time to respond to, and she needs to develop three others that are slated for next month. In addition, her supervisor has just asked her if she would serve on a special task force set up by the commissioner's office.

Personnel responsible for training often find themselves with too much to do just responding to requests for training activities and coping with the daily workload. It is difficult for many staff to develop formal training plans as called for in planning models, let alone find the time to do a well-thought-out needs analysis. The reality is that planning takes time, and there just may not be enough white space in a day's calendar to allow for adequate time to do it.

Organizational Environment

There are some organizations that are conducive to planning, and thus the use of a program planning model would be encouraged. There are other organizations that seem to run on a crisis mentality, always trying to solve the day's problems before the day is over. These same organizations may be short staffed and/or their staff may not be well organized. Trying to introduce the idea of using a program planning model, which calls for forward planning and thinking, may be almost impossible in such a climate.

Lack of Knowledge about Available Models

Many personnel involved with the training function are not aware of the models of program planning available for their use. This is not surprising because many training specialists are content specialists first and foremost and have not been exposed to materials related to program planning. Also, the resources for this type of personnel may not be easy to obtain because they are not readily available in their specialty area. Other personnel, who have only a peripheral involvement in training, have little time, and may not see the need, to become knowledgeable in this arena. In addition, many of the models are difficult to interpret and to use in any practical sense due to the way in which they are presented. The practitioner may not have the time necessary to plod through a more formal academic text, no matter how good the proposed model may be.

Rejection of Models as Too Confining To Be Helpful

The idea of using a program planning model is rejected by some training personnel because they view it as too confining to be helpful. This is especially so for the lock-step models of planning. For example, Joe S., a knowledgeable and experienced trainer, has tried to adapt at least two models into his every day work activities. But, he found that they just did not fit his situation. He was spending more time trying to rework the models themselves than on planning the actual programs. Thus he is back to his "good old seat of the pants" planning style because it has worked well for him in the past.

SUMMARY

1. Models of program planning come in all shapes and sizes. They may be simplistic in their orientation, with steps one through five, or they may be very complex, with highly developed flowcharts depicting a comprehensive array of decision points.
2. Five reasons why program planning models can be useful are:
   a. Resources are used more effectively
   b. Daily work is made easier
   c. Teamwork is fostered
   d. Basis for management control is provided
   e. Better programs are developed
3. There are four major reasons why staff involved with training programs do not use program planning models:
   a. Time pressures
   b. Organizational environment
   c. Lack of knowledge about available models
   d. Rejection of models as too confining to be helpful

1. List at least four reasons why using a model of program planning could be useful to you.

_____

_____

_____

_____

2. List at least three reasons why using a model of program planning would be difficult for you.

_____

_____

_____

3. Ask one or more of your coworkers to do the same process, and then compare your responses. Devise strategies, where appropriate, for how the difficulties in using a program planning model could be overcome. List these strategies.

_____

_____

_____

4

A CHECKLIST FOR PLANNING SUCCESSFUL PROGRAMS

Presented in this chapter is an overview of the model of program planning to be discussed in detail in Chapters 5 through 15 of this book. The model, as shown in Figure 4.1, consists of 12 components. Although the model appears to be sequential, it is really a set of interacting and dynamic elements (Houle, 1972). Most program planners work with a number of components at the same time and not necessarily in any standard order. For example, a trainer may begin to handle the program arrangements and logistics prior to ever deciding what the specific objectives of the program might be. This often happens when making facility arrangements for a major conference. The key word in using the model is flexibility. The use of the model should be tailored to meet the demands of a specific planning situation.

This model should be viewed as an open system. Thus outside factors can have an impact on the program design process, many of which are beyond the control of the planner (Nadler, 1982). In reality, a program planner can never know all the variables in the planning process and these variables might change during the planning stages. For example, in the midst of planning a major three-day workshop for mid-level managers, a trainer learned that a merger would be taking place a month before his planned program. This merger would mean not only a change in the people who might attend, but also a major revision of the objectives and content of the program.

FIGURE 4.1. Caffarella Model of Program Development[a]

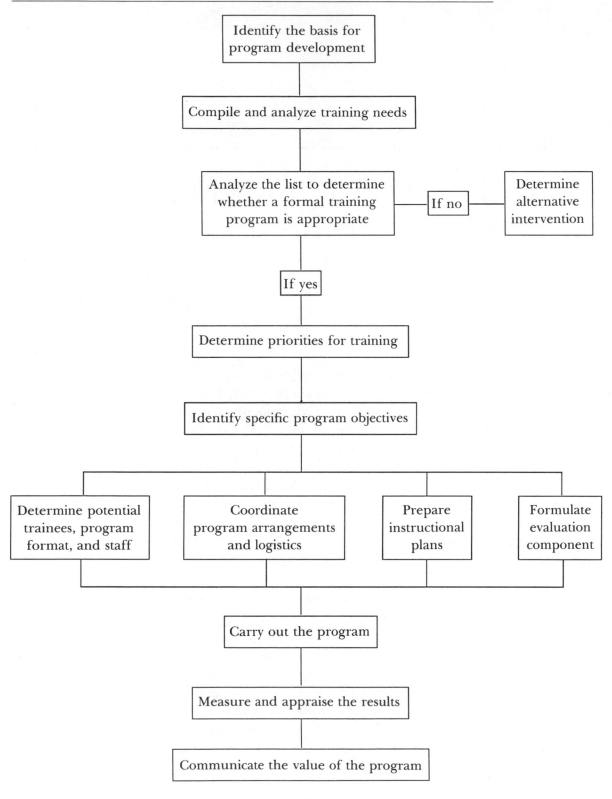

[a] The key word in using this model is flexibility.

SOURCES ON WHICH THE MODEL WAS BUILT

The model is derived from three major sources: systems theory, principles of adult learning, and practical experience. Systems theory provides the model's framework and was taken from Tyler's (1949) description of the curriculum development process. He outlined four major steps in the process: (1) define purpose, (2) specify objectives to guide the learning, (3) select method, and (4) evaluate to measure what has been learned. Five additional models (Houle, 1972; Knowles, 1980; Laird, 1985; Nadler, 1982; and Tracey, 1984) were also used as primary sources to further elaborate and develop the model. In addition, four secondary sources (Boyle, 1981; Gane, 1972; Kaufman and Stone, 1983; and Munson, 1984) provided some very useful material.

It was also important to consider how adults learn and change in the building of this model. Knowles (1980) and Boyle (1981) both stressed adult learning in their materials on program planning. More specifically, some of the major principles and practices of adult learning (Cross, 1981; Kidd, 1973; Knowles, 1980; Long, 1983; Smith, 1982; Tough, 1979, 1982; and Vogt, 1982) that were used in developing the model are outlined in the following list.

1. Adults can and do want to learn, regardless of their age.
2. Most adults tend to hold perceptions of themselves as independent and self-reliant people.
3. Adults have a rich background of experience. They tend to learn best when new information builds on past knowledge and experience.
4. Adults are motivated to learn based on a combination of complex internal and external forces. We need to understand the nature of those forces and how they interact to inhibit and/or encourage adults to learn.
5. Adults have different levels and styles of learning.
6. For the most part, adults are pragmatic in their learning. They tend to want to apply their learning to present situations.
7. Adults come to a learning situation with their own personal goals and objectives, which may or may not be the same as those given for the learning situation.
8. Adults appear to be better motivated to learn when they are actively involved in the learning process.
9. Much of the adult's learning tends to have an effect on others (e.g., work colleagues, subordinates, customers).
10. Adults learn best in situations that are both physically and psychologically comfortable.

Specific examples of how some of these principles and practices of how adults learn and change have been incorporated into the program development model and are shown in Table 4.1.

The third source used in developing the model was practical experience, my own and that of other professionals in the field. The importance of this source is demonstrated by the work of Pennington and Green (1976). They found in their research that the planning process consisted of a clear set of tasks and decisions. But, in comparing their findings with ideal models of program planning, major discrepancies emerged. For example, comprehensive needs assessments were rarely conducted, though this is seen as a major component of most program planning models. In addition, little indication was given that when designing actual instructional activities, such accepted variables as learner characteristics and learning outcomes, were regularly considered in the planning process. These findings were also used in the model presented.

Two groups of professionals provided some very helpful ideas on the practical usefulness of the model: (1) my graduate students (many of whom are practicing professionals) in human resource development and adult education; and (2) participants in a workshop I conducted on the model at the 1985 American Society for Training and Development National Conference in Anaheim, California. These ideas were incorporated in revising the model to its present form.

TASKS WITHIN EACH COMPONENT OF THE MODEL

Each program component includes a set of tasks and responsibilities. All of the tasks do not need to be addressed in developing every program. For example, once a solid basis for training and development activities is identified—strong management support and a clear statement of the training unit's mission—it will not need to be repeated for each new program. However, review of policy statements and support systems is helpful at specified intervals. The same could be said for the process of compiling a list of ideas, needs, and problems for possible training programs. One well-conceived and executed needs analysis can provide data pointing to a number of needed training programs and activities.

The tasks are presented in a program development checklist in Table 4.2. Each task is explored more fully in Chapters 5 through 15.

TABLE 4.1. Incorporating the Principles and Practices of How Adults Learn into Selected Components of the Caffarella Model of Program Development

Selected Components of the Program Development Model	Example of How To Integrate Principles and Practices of How Adults Learn into Selected Components
Identify the basis for program development	Training programs for adults should be based on the idea that adults can and do want to learn, regardless of age. They appear to learn best when the instructor and the learner are partners in the learning process. Learning programs should build on the accumulated knowledge and experience of the adult, and should also be practical, whenever appropriate. The learner should be involved in all stages of planning. These principles should be a part of the basic philosophy and practice of both the organization and program planner.
Compile and analyze training needs	Adults have their own learning agendas, related to their personal goals, and social roles (e.g., as worker, parent). It is therefore important to include the viewpoints of both individual learners and ideas from the systems (e.g., work, government) in which these individuals function.
Prepare specific instructional plans	Instructors should design their learning objective so participants, whenever possible, can incorporate their own learning agendas. The instructional content should build upon the past knowledge and experiences of the participants and be, where appropriate, problem-oriented and practical. Teaching techniques should permit active learner participation and provide opportunities to apply newly learned knowledge and skill. Learning activities should encourage participants to assume responsibility for their own learning and become active partners in the learning process.
Formulate evaluation component	Adults want to give and receive feedback on their learning experiences, both from a personal and programmatic standpoint. Thus opportunities for individual evaluation, by both the instructor and the learner, should be part of the evaluation plan.
Carry out the program	The learning climate should make adults feel respected, accepted, and supported. Instructors should provide opportunities for the participants to modify the training activity (e.g., changing objectives, content, methods). Evaluation data should be collected so as not to interfere with the learning or rights of participants.

TABLE 4.2. Program Development Checklist

Identify the Basis for Program Development

☐ Know the purpose of your organization, including present mission and future directions.

☐ Establish a base of support for the planning function.

☐ Spell out your philosophy of program development for adults, including your views about training, adults as learners, and the role of the trainer.

☐ Develop a formal mission statement for each training unit about the purposes and objectives of the unit.

Compile and Analyze Training Needs

☐ Conduct a formal needs assessment of present employees using a variety of techniques (e.g., task and job analyses, written questionnaires, telephone surveys).

☐ Respond to specific overall organizational needs for training (e.g., installation of microcomputers for all secretarial personnel, change in product or service, change in output levels).

☐ Use ideas generated from previous training programs.

☐ Review performance evaluation data.

☐ Respond to legislative mandates (e.g., affirmative action) and regulatory agencies (e.g., Occupational Safety and Health Administration).

☐ Review training programs from other organizations and prepackaged training programs from outside vendors.

☐ Seek suggestions from colleagues and associates.

☐ Search relevant professional literature.

Analyze the List To Determine Whether
a Formal Training Program Is Appropriate

☐ If no, determine alternative interventions.

☐ If yes, screen and prioritize the remaining items.

Prioritize Needs/Ideas/Problems for Training Programs

☐ Make explicit your assumptions underlying the planning process.

☐ Decide on personnel to do the screening and prioritizing process.

☐ Screen the needs/ideas/problems through four filters: (1) institutional purpose, (2) interests of supervisors of potential participants, (3) interests of potential participants, and (4) feasibility of the program.

☐ Prioritize the program/needs/ideas that should be implemented and set up a master schedule for implementing them.

TABLE 4.2. Program Development Checklist (*continued*)

Identify Specific Program Objectives

☐ State the intended results of the program, including the expected impact on individuals (with type and number of people) and/or organizational units.

☐ Check to see that the program objectives are written in practical and concrete terms and that they will be understood by all the parties involved (e.g., participants, trainers, management).

Determine Potential Trainees, Program Format, and Staff

☐ Choose the content of the program and of the various subsections.

☐ Determine potential trainees and do a target population analysis.

☐ Choose the most appropriate program format (e.g., individualized, small or large group).

☐ Determine overall program length, times for individual sessions and subsections of the program, and potential dates.

☐ Identify staff and outline their roles (e.g., program coordinator, instructor, evaluator).

Coordinate Program Arrangements and Logistics

☐ Prepare a program budget.

☐ Obtain needed facilities and equipment.

☐ Obtain, as needed, final management approval and/or support for the program.

☐ Market the program.

*Prepare Specific Instructional Plan in Cooperation
with the Individual Instructor/Facilitator*

☐ Define the specific role(s) of the instructors and facilitators.

☐ Define specific learning objectives for each training activity.

☐ Select and sequence content.

☐ Choose instructional techniques.

☐ Select instructional materials and aids.

☐ Develop an evaluation component for each learning activity.

☐ Prepare an instructional plan.

(*continued*)

TABLE 4.2. Program Development Checklist (continued)

Formulate a Continuous Program Evaluation Component

☐ Identify the individuals to be involved in planning and overseeing the evaluation.

☐ Define precisely the purpose of the evaluation and how the results will be used.

☐ Specify what outcomes will be judged and formulate the evaluation questions.

☐ Determine who will supply the evidence you will need (e.g., participants, instructors, training staff).

☐ Specify the evaluation design.

☐ Determine what techniques you will use to collect evaluation data.

☐ Specify the analysis procedures you will be using.

☐ Specify what criteria you will use in making judgements about the program.

☐ Determine the time framework and budget needed to conduct the evaluation.

Carry Out the Program

☐ Oversee all the program arrangements (e.g., registration, equipment, rooms, meals).

☐ Create a positive climate for learning.

☐ Provide a system for monitoring the program and revise the activities as needed.

☐ Gather needed data for evaluation and record keeping.

☐ Award certificates or other appropriate recognition to the participants.

☐ Tie up all loose ends after the program is completed (e.g., store extra materials, check equipment).

Measure and Appraise the Results of the Program

☐ Analyze the evaluation data.

☐ Interpret the data and generate conclusions.

☐ Formulate program recommendations.

☐ Use this data to make decisions about new or revised training activities or alternative interventions.

Communicate the Value of the Program to Appropriate Publics

☐ Prepare a report on the program.

☐ Communicate this report to key individuals and groups.

☐ Follow up as needed with appropriate individuals and groups to clarify questions or concerns about the program.

ASSUMPTIONS MADE IN USING THE MODEL

This model rests on five major assumptions. Each of these assumptions has been drawn primarily from the work of Houle (1972) and Knowles (1980).

Assumption One. A training program should focus on what the participants actually learn and how this learning results in a change in the participants' knowledge level, performance, and/or attitudes.

Program planners must have a clear understanding of why they are doing what they are doing. They should be able to demonstrate that some sort of change has come about as a result of the training program. This change may be knowledge acquisition, skills development, improved job performance, and/or specific attitude adjustments. Such changes can be documented in a number of ways, from measuring and appraising changes in individual learners to evaluating changes in production.

Assumption Two. Designing training programs is a practical art.

There is no single method of planning training programs that will ensure success. Rather, a program planner is very much like an orchestra conductor. He or she must be able to bring together diverse players and pieces in an harmonious and balanced effort. This may not be easy because some of the pieces may be much more difficult than anticipated and some of the players may not be as adept at their parts as was hoped.

Assumption Three. Developing training programs is a cooperative versus an "operative" endeavor.

There must be cooperation between the learners and planners in developing and implementing a successful program. Such cooperation may take several forms, from informally screening a proposed program or specific instructional model through a group of potential participants, to involving those participants in a formal planning team for the entire programming process.

Assumption Four. The development of any training program is a complex interaction of tasks, people, and events.

Developing training programs very rarely works in a completely logical fashion. Planners tend to spend a great deal of time in formulating and then reformulating the many facets of the process. In addition, the more persons that you add to the planning process, the less logical that process tends to be. For example, when different people are responsible for different parts of a program, some people may make every planning deadline while others never do. The latter can be a planner's nightmare, especially if the delinquent person's task is an essential element in getting the program off the ground. The key to keeping oneself sane as a program planner is to maintain flexibility throughout the process.

Assumption Five. An individual, using one or more planning model guides, can learn to be a more effective program planner through practice.

Effective program planners are not born that way. Through trial and error, they become more skilled at balancing the various components of the process. It is important for planners to evaluate their planning efforts to see where they have been effective and where they can improve.

SUMMARY

1. An overview of a 12-component model of program planning, to be discussed in Chapters 5 through 15 of this book, was given. The model was presented as a set of interacting and dynamic elements, with the key word for using the model being flexibility.
2. This program planning model is derived from three major sources: systems theory, principles of adult learning, and practical experience.
3. The major principles and practices of adult learning used in developing the model are reviewed. Examples of these include:
   a. Adults can and do want to learn, regardless of age.
   b. Most adults tend to hold perceptions of themselves as independent and self-reliant people.
   c. Adults have a rich background of experience. They tend to learn best when new information builds on past knowledge and experience.
4. Each of the 12 program components has its own set of tasks and responsibilities. Not all of the tasks need to be addressed in developing each individual program. A program development checklist listing each of the tasks is outlined.

5. This model rests on five major assumptions:
    a. A training program should focus on what the participants actually learn and how this learning results in a change in the participants' knowledge level, performance, and/or attitudes.
    b. Designing training programs is a practical art.
    c. Developing training programs is a cooperative versus an "operative" endeavor.
    d. The development of any training program is a complex interaction of tasks, people, and events.
    e. An individual, using one or more planning models as guides, can learn to be a more effective program planner through practice.

5

IDENTIFYING THE BASIS
FOR PROGRAM DEVELOPMENT

Three major tasks emerge as essential in identifying and establishing a basis for program development in an organization: (1) becoming knowledgeable about the overall mission, present operations, and future directions of your organization; (2) establishing a solid base of support for training activities; and (3) identifying a personal philosophy related to program development for the adult learner. In addition, directors of formal training divisions need a clear mission statement describing the purposes and objectives of specific units. The way that training personnel tackle each of these tasks will differ depending on whether the training function is centralized or decentralized, large or small, and is well-accepted or marginal within the organization.

BECOMING KNOWLEDGEABLE
ABOUT YOUR ORGANIZATION

Personnel who develop training programs cannot work in a vacuum. They need to have a basic understanding of their organization (Johnson, 1976; Munson, 1984). This includes a clear idea of the overall mission or purpose and the proposed future directions of the organization. In addition, training staff need to be well-versed about the operation of their own unit and how that unit relates to the overall mission of the organization.

Where can this information be found? Two basic sources are usually accessible to employees of most organizations: (1) written documents (e.g., annual reports, organizational white papers, strategic planning reports), and (2) talking with people (e.g., colleagues, supervisors, key managers). In addition, the planner may have access to the executive dining room for informal lunches, attend meetings with top management personnel, and/or be invited to key committee meetings.

The level and depth of the knowledge a person needs to have about an organization varies depending on the training assignment. Let us consider two very different situations.

SITUATION ONE. Mary C. has just been appointed as a training specialist for computer operations in the commercial division of Jones Bank. A new operating system is to be brought on-line within the next six months. Mary will be responsible both for developing the user manuals and conducting the actual training of employees. She has been promoted through the ranks to her present position and has a clear understanding of how her unit presently functions.

In addition, her supervisor has briefed her on the proposed changes and their importance to both the commercial division and the general operation of the bank. The supervisor has also explained to Mary the changing nature of commercial banking, and especially how their bank is changing. Mary obtains for review a copy of the last two years' annual reports and some white papers on the commercial division to better understand her particular situation.

SITUATION TWO. Fred D. has just assumed the position of corporate vice president for human resource development and training for the Jones Bank. Though familiar with the banking industry, he was hired from the outside. Fred had done his homework prior to his interview. He has a very clear "outsider's understanding" of the overall mission and future directions of the bank based on written materials and his interviews. Now he needs to convert that data to an insider's perspective. Fred has decided on three basic strategies to achieve those ends: (1) review all available in-house documents related to the present and future operations of the organization; (2) interview members of the top management team, key middle managers of each major division of the bank, and his own staff; and (3) attend all strategic planning meetings, at both the corporate and division levels. Fred hopes through his efforts to gain an in-depth understanding of his new organization and how his unit fits into that organization.

Both Mary and Fred needed to gain a basic understanding of the organization in which they work. But the type and level of knowledge that each person needed to function was quite different.

ESTABLISH A SOLID BASE OF SUPPORT FOR PLANNING AND CONDUCTING TRAINING ACTIVITIES

It is important to establish a firm base of support for planning and conducting training programs. Nadler (1982) stresses that this support must come in both commitment and action. He sees commitment as a promise, which usually is in the form of a speech or other verbal statement, while action is actual involvement in the training function.

Munson (1984) says support must come from three major groups: top management, the immediate supervisors of potential training participants, and the trainees themselves. The reasons why these three groups are important, and strategies for involving each group, are outlined in the next three subsections.

Support from Top Management

Both Munson (1984) and Nadler (1982) stress the importance of securing support for training from top management. They decide whether training is an integral part of the operation, and how in general it will be carried out. Top management's support is reflected by budgetary commitments, their style and practice of management (including their view of personal career development), and their public support of the training function in organizational publications and key organizational meetings (Munson, 1984).

Top management support is gained in a number of ways, including involving them in the training process. Suggested ideas primarily from Munson (1984) and Nadler (1982) are:

1. First and foremost: do good work! Set specific goals and objectives for the training activities and then meet them. Provide proof, in an easily understood form, of the successful results.

2. Request that top management issue formal policy and procedural statements concerning the training function. Such management actions might include (Nadler, 1982, pp. 230–232):

>   Requires attendance at training for certain categories of employees
>
>   Authorizes release time or changed work hours to allow participation in training
>
>   Authorizes production differentials for trainees for short periods back on the job

Issues statements on new performance levels expected following training

Approves use of confidential organizational data as resources for training

3. Ask selected top executives to become actively involved in the design and evaluation of training programs. For example, a manager could serve as a consultant to a planning group designing a program in an area of his or her competence; or a group of managers could serve in an ad hoc capacity to preview proposed training programs that have organizational wide impact.

Munson (1984) warns that it is easy to get discouraged trying to gain the support of top management. It can take a considerable investment of time with few initial concrete results. Yet time may be one the keys in gaining this group's support. As training activities are usually not the focus of most organizations, it will take longer for top executives to take note of such activities and to give them more than nominal support. Thus, it is important to develop a track record of successful training activities.

Support from the Immediate Supervisors of Potential Training Participants

Support from the immediate supervisors of potential training participants is crucial at all points in the training cycle, from preplanning to follow-up. To illustrate, consider the following case.

THE NO-SHOWS. The enrollment of supervisory personnel for the training seminars on communication skills is always good. But, on the day of the training session, there is always a high percentage of "no-shows" and attendees who wander in and out of the session. Despite this, participants consistently rate the program very high, especially in usefulness for on-the-job activities. In investigating this problem, it is discovered that for a period of one year the "no-shows" and "leave-earlys" have all come from 4 of the 10 departments involved in the program. It is also noted that the managers in two of these four departments have complained loudly and often about the enormous amount of time their people requested for training activities.

As can be seen by this scenario, supervisors have influence over whether employees can attend training sessions. Also, supervisors play a very important part in whether or not any of the new knowledge and skills acquired in training is translated by employees into a change in job performance. If supervisors understand and support the objectives of the training efforts, it is easier for employees to change their behavior and also for supervisors to reinforce that change positively.

As with top management, support for training activities from the immediate supervisor of the proposed trainees can be gained in a number of ways. Table 5.1, based on Nadler (1982) and Broad (1980), shows supportive actions supervisors could become involved in before, during, and after training activities.

Although all aspects of the training process are important, it is of greatest importance in working with supervisors to seek their active involvement before and after training. Special attention should be paid to assist supervisors in working with their employees on integrating training information and skills into actual on-the-job activities. This can be a very time-consuming activity, but very beneficial to all parties involved—the trainer, the trainee, and the supervisor.

TABLE 5.1. Ways in Which Immediate Supervisors Can Be Actively Involved in the Training Process

Before Training	During Training	After Training
Assist in the assessment of the learning needs of employees, including asking them what they perceive their needs to be.	Participate in the actual training sessions as appropriate.	Work with trainees to assist them in integrating the knowledge and skills learned to actual on-the-job activities.
Participate in planning a program appropriate for employees.	Serve as an instructor or resource person in a training session.	Reinforce the use of new knowledge and skills learned on a regular, planned basis.
Assist in scheduling training activities.	Avoid calling trainees out of sessions to work on job-related problems.	Provide time for trainees to share their learning with fellow employees.
Choose the employees to be involved in training activities.	Award certificates to participants who complete a training activity.	Assist in collecting data for evaluation and follow-up.
Work with trainees to help them prepare for the upcoming session, with the focus on how the training material can be integrated back on the job.		
Assist in collecting baseline data for evaluation and follow-up.		

Support from Trainees

Support from trainees is also important, as highlighted by Munson (1984). They make their influence felt before, during, and after training. If a training activity is good, trainees will let their co-workers know. If a training program is bad, they will probably be even more vocal about it with their colleagues. Thus attendance at future training activities is definitely influenced by former training participants.

How training participants view potential training events can also be influenced by their co-workers. Are the potential trainees committed as a group to changing their job performance as a result of training; or do they view the training sessions more as a chance to get away from the work piled up on their desks? If the majority of the participants have the latter attitude, it can make the training sessions, and follow-up studies, very difficult. This problem can be complicated by such factors as "we were all made to come," and "we do not believe any of this stuff is really very worthwhile."

Pressure from co-workers can also be a powerful factor in whether a trainee can actually change any of his daily job practices. For example, Jane, a secretary in a large department, had learned what she believed to be a more effective way of logging incoming calls. Excitedly, she told her fellow secretaries about it over coffee. They all groaned and told her that it would just make more work for them. Because Jane's boss was not especially interested in the new system, she decided to drop the whole idea. On the other hand, Sue, a secretary in an adjacent department, had convinced her office mates that the new logging system was really better. With this support from her peers, she asked her boss if she could have some job time to train the other secretaries in the department. Her boss readily agreed.

Support from trainees is best produced by giving worthwhile and useful training programs (Munson, 1984). Trainees will quickly spread the word that program A or B was well-presented and helpful to them in their work. Also, a number of the strategies presented in Table 5.1 for involving immediate supervisors in the training process can be extended to trainees. Examples of additional strategies for gaining the support of trainees are outlined in Table 5.2.

FORMAL SUPPORT STRUCTURE: THE USE OF COMMITTEES

Using committees can be a helpful way to build support for the training function. These committees may be permanent or put together on an ad hoc basis as needed. Whatever the form, purpose, function, and

TABLE 5.2. Ways in Which Trainees Can Be Involved in the Training Process, Other Than as Participants

Before Training	During Training	After Training
Ask the trainees what they believe their job performance training needs are.	Invite trainees to serve as instructors and/or resource persons.	Encourage trainees to share the information/skills they have learned with their co-workers.
Invite selected trainees to assist in planning training activities.	At specified intervals, ask the trainees how they feel the sessions are going, making changes as appropriate based on their suggestions.	Ask the trainees whether they feel they can use what they have learned in their jobs, and why.
Have the trainees outline how they believe the training session might help them in their work.	At the close of the training activities, have the trainees outline ways to use what they have learned back on the job.	

authority of a committee must be understood by those involved. Further guidelines for the successful operation of committees, abstracted from Knowles (1980), are given in Table 5.3.

The Training Committee

One common type of committee is a formally constituted training committee. Although these committees are usually advisory and thus not empowered to make decisions, committee members can nonetheless influence staff and affect the direction and form of the training function in an organization.

Lauffer (1978) stresses that members of training committees need to have real tasks to do. Knowles (1980) has outlined tasks appropriate for such a committee:

1. Identify current organizational problems for which training might offer solutions
2. Assist in designing and carrying out a needs assessment
3. Establish priorities for training activities

4. Assist in formulating broad goals and objectives for the training function

5. Interpret past achievements and efforts to appropriate people (e.g., top management, consumers, supervisors)

6. Contribute ideas to the planning of specific training activities

7. Serve as talent scouts for new instructors and resource people

8. Assist in implementing training activities (e.g., registering participants, serving as instructor)

9. Help in evaluating the training function

TABLE 5.3. Guiding Principles for the Operation of Committees

Factors	Principles
Purpose and objectives	Committee members should understand clearly what they are to do and what their powers are.
Focus	Committee members should work on solutions to existing problems, and not merely rubber-stamp already worked-out solutions.
Meetings	The agenda for committee meetings should concern problems of importance to committee members and staff associated with the committee.
Feedback	Committee members should receive feedback on their work as committee members, both individually and as a group.
Involvement with programs	Committee members should become involved in training activities, including actual training events and ceremonial ones.
Administrative details	Administrative details of committee work (e.g., meeting notices, handouts, minutes) should be handled smoothly and efficiently by staff and not left to committee members.
Evaluation	Committee members should periodically evaluate their work from both an individual and group perspective.
Individual responsibilities, tasks	Individual and small group responsibilities accepted by committee members should be clear, specific, and definitive. A tracking system, administered by committee members, should be set up to ensure that all assignments are carried out in a timely and effective manner.

Choosing members for the training committee requires careful deliberation. Three major factors to be considered are:

1. Types of people needed (e.g., experts, organizational leaders, consumers)
2. Individual characteristics (e.g., age, sex, ethnic background)
3. Geographic location, especially for regional and national operations

One way to ensure these specific factors are taken into account in choosing members is to use a two-way grid, adapted from the work of Houle (1960), as portrayed in Table 5.4.

TABLE 5.4. Two-Way Grid for Selecting Training Committee Members

Criteria	Present Committee Members						Potential Committee Members			
	1	2	3	4	5	6	a	b	c	d
Age										
Under 30 years of age	x			x						
From 30 to 45 years of age		x	x							
Over 45 years of age					x	x				
Sex										
Men	x				x	x				
Women		x	x	x						
Ethnic origin										
Caucasian			x	x	x	x				
Black	x									
Hispanic		x								
Other										
Types of personnel needed										
Subject experts		x		x						
Process experts	x		x							
Organizational leaders				x						
Consumers					x					
Geographic location of members										
Local office			x	x	x					
Regional office	x									
Corporate office		x								
General community		x								

SOURCE: Adapted from "Grid for Selecting Board Members," in Cyril O. Houle, *The Effective Board.* Copyright 1960 by Cambridge Book Company, 888 7th Avenue, New York, NY 10106. Reprinted with permission of the publisher.

In addition to these three major factors, Knowles (1980, pp. 76–77) has stressed that

> *care must be taken to select individuals who not only represent something, but who will be effective, and such personal qualities must be kept in mind . . . as the following:*
> *1) Interest in the program and its objectives;*
> *2) Willingness to serve;*
> *3) Competence or educability for the work of the committee;*
> *4) Availability for the work, in terms of time, health, strength and convenience of location;*
> *5) Ability to work with other members of the committee;*
> *6) Position of influence with significant elements of the "organization/community."*

Ad Hoc Committees

An ad hoc committee or task force is usually constituted for a short time. Its role is generally limited to accomplishing specific tasks, with very clear and explicit responsibilities. Committee members usually only advise on specific matters, rather than becoming involved in their implementation (Lauffer, 1978).

One of the most common uses for ad hoc committees is in developing specific training activities. For example, Fred R., a central staff training coordinator, is asked to develop a program for secretarial staff on "Organizing Your Work." Although "canned" programs are available, he has not been impressed with those he has reviewed. Thus he decides to develop an in-house training program. Although he has already conducted secretarial training in various content areas, he feels he would like some assistance in planning this particular program. He asks four people to join an ad hoc planning committee to help him: two office managers, a secretary at grade three and one at grade five. All of his committee members are well-respected by their fellow workers and are known as top-notch personnel. Fred has requested that the group meet at least three times to discuss program content and how the activities should be structured. All the committee members receive permission from their supervisors to be on the committee and are delighted by the invitation.

Another reason for constituting an ad hoc committee is to support a large training project within an organization. Such projects may range from an organizational wide training needs assessment to instituting a major new method for training, such as computer-based instruction. It is mandatory for such ad hoc committees to enlist the support of key line personnel, including top management when desirable. For example, an ad hoc committee appointed to oversee a corporate-wide needs assessment of all sales personnel should include the following types of players (titles, of course, vary among organizations):

Committee Members

Vice president for marketing and sales, corporate office

Regional sales managers

Sales managers, district office

Top direct sales personnel (representing different experience levels in terms of time on job and types of sales territory)

Ex-Officio Members

Corporate-level training staff (to serve as staff support for the committee)

Such a variety of personnel ensures that the picture of the training needs of sales personnel is clear and accurate, and that programs developed in response to identified needs will be well-received. The actual committee members, representing the best and the brightest in the sales force must, of course, be chosen with care.

IDENTIFYING A PERSONAL PHILOSOPHY RELATED TO PROGRAM DEVELOPMENT

Boyle (1981) points out the importance of identifying one's own personal beliefs and values concerning the process of program development. He provides a framework to assist the trainer in ordering these beliefs, which is displayed in Table 5.5.

TABLE 5.5. Framework for Identifying a Personal Philosophy of Program Development

Beliefs	Examples of Belief Statements
About the purpose of training	The purpose of training is to increase the productivity of workers.
	The purpose of training is to ensure a satisfied work force.
	The purpose of training is to assist workers in acquiring the information and skills necessary to be more effective and efficient.
About the learner	Trainees can and do want to learn, regardless of age.
	Trainees tend to see themselves as independent and self-reliant.
	Trainees want to learn useful and practical information/skills that they can use back in their work situation.
About teaching	Trainees are motivated to learn by being actively involved in the learning process.
	Trainees and instructors are partners in the training process.
	Trainees learn best when new information builds on past knowledge and experiences.
About the process of program development	Prospective trainees and their supervisors should be involved in all phases of program development.
	The needs of the organization should always take precedence over those of trainees.

Rarely do persons involved with training ever fully articulate their personal philosophy on program planning; yet a system of beliefs guide their actions. Contrast, for example, two different persons responsible for developing training activities. Bob C. involves as many people as possible in designing the training activities for which he is responsible. He has a very active training committee and uses a variety of ad hoc groups in the planning of new programs and other training initiatives. He strongly advises his instructors to use participatory methods in their program delivery and to gear their material to what would be useful to the trainees back on the job. He ensures that all trainees receive prompt feedback on what they have learned, whether it be information, skills, or changes in attitudes.

Wanda R., on the other hand, plans most of her training activities by herself, or with one or two of her staff. She occasionally hires outside consultants to assist. She finds working with committees and especially staff outside her unit very cumbersome. She does not like her instructors

TABLE 5.6. Different Philosophies of Program Development as Illustrated by Two Training Personnel

Beliefs	Bob C.	Wanda R.
About the purpose of training	The purpose of training is to increase knowledge, develop skills, and/or change attitudes related to a person's work.	The purpose of training is to produce behavioral change in job performance.
About the learner	Trainees want to learn useful and practical knowledge and skills they can apply to their work situations.	Trainees must be willing to change their work behavior as a result of training sessions.
About teaching	Trainees and instructors should be partners in the learning process. Learning should be an active process.	Instruction should be content-centered, with the instructor controlling the session at all times.
About the process of program development	Potential trainees and their supervisors should be involved in all phases of program development.	Training programs should be developed by experts on content and process.

to waste any time in class and requests that they stick strictly to the topic at hand. Although feedback is given to trainees related to the training they have received, it is sporadic and not very timely. She does attempt to measure if there has been any behavior change on the job, but not very successfully.

It appears, at least on the surface, that Bob C. and Wanda R. have different philosophies about program development as illustrated in Table 5.6.

In summary, people's underlying beliefs and values do affect the way they plan and carry out training activities.

DEVELOPMENT OF A MISSION STATEMENT FOR DEPARTMENTS OF TRAINING

Directors of training divisions need to have a clear mission statement outlining the overall purposes and functions of their training unit (Johnson, 1976; Munson, 1984). In setting up new training departments, writing this basic policy statement should be one of the first steps. The mission statement should address the "why, what, who, and where" of the operation.

Why?

Outlines the end result to be accomplished in terms of overall purpose.

What?

Describes the broad functional areas with which the training unit will be concerned.

Who?

Identifies the potential clientele with whom training staff work.

Where?

Describes the parameters of where the training unit will function (e.g., corporate level, divisional level, companywide).

For an example of a mission statement, see Table 5.7.

The mission statement should be approved by top management prior to its circulation among organizational personnel. Once it is approved, care should be taken that all appropriate individuals (e.g., division directors, supervisory personnel) receive a copy. This will ensure that key staff receive at least some basic information about the overall scope and responsibilities of the training unit.

TABLE 5.7. Sample of a Basic Mission Statement

The XYZ Organization Mission Statement for
Department of Training and Development

PURPOSE

The purpose of the Department of Training and Development is to "contribute toward the improved performance of human resources on the job and thereby contribute to the profitable growth of the organization" (Munson, 1984, p. 35).

FUNCTIONS

The staff of the Department of Training and Development are responsible for three primary functions:
1. To coordinate all existing training activities within the XYZ Organization;
2. To develop and manage all training activities for supervisory and management-level personnel; and
3. To serve as consultants to senior management on issues related to organizational change and development.

CLIENTELE AND ORGANIZATIONAL BASE

The clientele include managers and employees throughout the XYZ Organization. This includes corporate staff and personnel located within all divisions and locations of the organization. The staff of the Department of Training and Development work primarily with the training personnel located within each division and with management and supervisory personnel. Only the senior training staff serve as consultants to top management.

SUMMARY

1. Personnel who develop training programs cannot work in a vacuum. They need to have a basic understanding of their organization. This includes a clear idea of the overall mission or purpose and the proposed future directions of the organization. In addition, training staff need to be well-versed about the operation of their own unit and how that unit relates to the overall mission of the organization.

2. It is important to establish a firm basis of support for planning and conducting training programs. This support must come from three major groups: top management, the immediate supervisors of potential training participants, and the trainees themselves.

3. Using committees can be a helpful way to build support for the training function. These committees may be permanent (e.g., a training advisory committee) or they may be put together on an ad hoc basis as needed. Whatever the form, the purpose, function, and authority of the committee must be understood by those involved.

4. A four-component framework is provided to assist training personnel in identifying their own personal philosophy concerning program development:
   a. Beliefs about the purpose of training
   b. Beliefs about the learner
   c. Beliefs about teaching
   d. Beliefs about the process of program development

5. Directors of training divisions need to have a clear mission statement outlining the overall purposes and functions of their training units. The mission statement should address the "why, what, who, and where" of the operation.

1. List how you would investigate the mission of your organization using written documents and personal interviews. Be specific as to what documents you would want to review and whom you would want to interview.

   Documents To Review

   _____

   _____

   _____

   _____

   Persons To Interview

   _____

   _____

   _____

   _____

2. Based on your investigation, outline the overall present mission and proposed future directions of your organization.

   Present Mission

   _____

   _____

   _____

   _____

Proposed Future Directions

_____

_____

_____

_____

3. Outline how the program development activities in which you are presently involved fit in with the overall goals and future direction of your organization. Be as specific as possible.

_____

_____

_____

_____

_____

▶ CHAPTER 5, WORKSHEET 2: BUILDING A BASE OF SUPPORT FOR YOUR TRAINING PROGRAM

Complete the chart with ideas for how you could involve supervisors and potential trainees in your organization's training activities. Be as specific as possible in naming the persons and/or types of personnel you would like to include.

	Before Training		During Training		After Training	
	Activities	Potential Players	Activities	Potential Players	Activities	Potential Players
What super-visors could do						
What poten-tial train-ees could do						

► CHAPTER 5, WORKSHEET 3:
IDENTIFYING YOUR PERSONAL PHILOSOPHY OF
PROGRAM DEVELOPMENT

First identify your own beliefs in the following four areas. Then outline specific work actions that illustrate your belief statements as well as those that appear to contradict those statements.

Beliefs	Personal Belief Statement(s)	Your Work Actions that Illustrate Your Beliefs	Your Work Actions that Appear to Contradict Your Beliefs
About the purpose of training			
About the learner			
About teaching			
About the process of program development			

6

COMPILING AND ANALYZING
TRAINING NEEDS

John B. is not quite sure why the training activities he is coordinating are not, as his boss terms it, "overly successful." He has hired what he believes are top-flight instructors and has even included a free lunch as part of the training day. Yet overall, the enrollments are low and a small but noticeable number of participants leave at the coffee break. Participant evaluations, at least for those programs he remembers to have participants evaluate, praise the presenters and the food, but are critical about the usefulness and practicality of the information presented. John cannot understand this reaction because the training programs are exactly like those that one of his close friends, a training specialist at a similar organization, is running and his friend has received rave reviews for them. Perhaps, John thinks, he should talk to some of the participants, or their supervisors, to figure out why they are not appreciating his efforts.

For a successful training program, the needs and interests of the population must be considered (Boyle, 1981; Caffarella, 1982; Knowles, 1980; Laird, 1985; Tracey, 1984). This means being aware of the needs of potential trainees, their supervisors, upper-level management, and the organization as a whole (Giegold and Grindle, 1983; Knowles, 1980; Nadler, 1982; Tracey, 1984). Thus one of the major tasks of personnel involved with training is to compile a list of needs and ideas for training activities.

Generating this list can be done in a variety of ways, from conducting a formal needs analysis to responding to a request from a specific unit to assist with the training of line staff on some newly installed equipment.

WHAT ARE YOU LOOKING FOR?

An educational need is usually defined as a discrepancy or gap between what presently is and what should be (Beatty, 1981; Kaufman and Stone, 1983; Laird, 1985; Witkin, 1984). This gap can appear in many forms. It may be a gap in desired versus actual productivity; a discrepancy between what supervisors want their people to do and how they actually perform; or employees' perceptions of a lack of knowledge or skill in contrast to what they believe they should know or be able to do.

For the most part, training needs are performance related, such as helping employees do their present jobs better, orienting new employees, and keeping employees informed of technical and procedural changes (Employee Training, 1986; Laird, 1985; Moore and Dutton, 1978; Warren, 1979). Some training activities also provide an opportunity for employees to develop their own personal skills and knowledge, usually in concert with the performance-related needs, (Employee Training, 1986).

Laird (1985) has outlined two classes of training needs: micro and macro needs. "A micro training need exists for just one person, or for a very small population. Macro training needs exist in a large group of employees—frequently in the entire populations with the same job classification" (Laird, 1985, p. 49). Examples of micro and macro training needs are:

Micro Training Needs	Macro Training Needs
A new employee needs to understand what is expected of him or her on the job.	Orienting all employees when a new building is opened.
A three-person unit in the organization has microcomputers installed and all three are expected to know how to operate them.	All employees are expected to be able to use a newly installed companywide computer system.
A supervisor is having problems managing his or her time.	All first-line supervisors have been requested to initiate performance appraisal discussions in their units.

Both micro and macro needs must be considered when planning training activities, although how the training will be conducted may vary considerably between these two classes of needs.

SOURCES OF TRAINING NEEDS

Training needs are generated from three primary sources: people, the job, and the organization. Examples of specific sources, drawn primarily from the work of Laird (1985), Nadler (1982), and Tracey (1984), are given in Table 6.1.

TABLE 6.1. Sources of Training Needs

Source	Internal to Organization	External to Organization
People		
Individuals	Potential trainees	Trainers in other organizations
	Supervisors	Outside consultants
	Upper-level managers	
	Training personnel	
Groups	Job function groups (e.g., supervisors)	Professional and trade association
	Task function groups (e.g., top management)	Publishers of training materials
Job Specific	Personnel changes (e.g., new hires, promotions)	Professional and trade associations
	Job task changes	Outside consultants
	Changes in performance standards	Government regulations
	Equipment changes	
	Analyses of efficiency indexes (e.g., waste, down time, repairs, quality control)	
Organizational	Changes in mission of the organization	Government regulations and legislative mandate
	Mergers and acquisitions	Outside consultants
	Change in organizational structure	Pressure from outside competition
	New products/services	Environmental pressures (e.g., political, economic, demographic, technological)
	Analysis of organizational climate (e.g., grievances, absenteeism, turnover, accidents)	

61

Often the first sign that training might be needed surfaces as a specific problem from one of the three primary sources (Gane, 1972; Michalak and Yager, 1979; Nadler, 1982).

1. *People*

Salespeople comment to their boss that they are not receiving telephone messages in a timely fashion, which is affecting their relationships with customers.

A number of mid-level managers have voiced concern over adequate support services for their personnel.

2. *Job Specific*

Shift one consistently produces more computer boards than shifts two and three.

A large number of the secretarial staff are having difficulty using their newly installed word-processing system.

3. *Organizational*

There is a higher rate of absenteeism for Division X than for Divisions Y and Z.

On a companywide basis supervisors appear to be having trouble interpreting to their subordinates the new set of policies and procedures concerning overtime work.

At this point the job of the trainer is to define the problem in more depth. He or she must decide whether the problem is:

1. Performance related
2. Short or long term
3. New or recurring
4. Affecting a few or many employees
5. Urgent, important, or unimportant

This process of problem clarification and analysis is often done through a formal and/or informal needs assessment.

GATHERING DATA

Although most models of program planning advocate completing a formal needs assessment, this is only one of many ways to generate ideas and needs for training programs. In a recent study completed by the American Society of Training and Development (ASTD), about half of the training executives indicated that this process is not done most of the time in their organizations. "Interestingly, the frequency of needs assessment declines with the job level for which the training program is being developed" (Employee Training, 1986, p. 35).

> SCENARIO ONE. Matt C. attended a workshop on "Motivating the Experienced Employee" hosted by the local ASTD chapter. He believed the ideas presented would be very helpful to his first-line supervisory staff. He first reviewed the materials he received at the workshop, including previewing two suggested films he had not previously seen. He then tried out the idea over lunch with three key supervisors and they were enthusiastic about the proposed program.

> SCENARIO TWO. Joyce R., a training specialist for a large paper company, has been informed that the level of productivity on two pieces of newly installed equipment has been steadily declining, even though there was an initial production rise a month after the machines were fully operating. After closely examining the analysis of efficiency indexes (e.g., down time, repairs, waste), she decides, in consultation with two of her line supervisors, to do a formal job analysis to get a better handle on the problem. Joyce forms an ad hoc task force to assist her.

Whether the generation of ideas and needs is formal or informal, it is important to consider all sources of those needs: people, job-related, and organizational.

CONDUCTING A FORMAL NEEDS ASSESSMENT

A formal needs assessment is a systematic way to identify educational deficiencies or problems. The focus of the assessment is not on solutions for specific problems but on clarifying and defining the problems.

There is no one accepted process for conducting a formal needs assessment, particularly in choosing which methods or techniques to use. Rather, a number of models or descriptions have been developed (Caffarella, 1982; Gane, 1972; Kaufman and Stone, 1983; Michalak and

Yager, 1979; Witkin, 1984). A revised version of Caffarella's model is used to illustrate the process (Caffarella, 1982, pp. 6–7).

There are 10 steps involved in this formal needs assessment process. The steps are outlined in Table 6.2, with a specific example given for each step relating to a needs assessment for mid-level managers.

TABLE 6.2. Steps Involved in a Formal Needs Assessment Process

Steps	Example
1. Make a conscious decision to complete a needs assessment with a commitment to planning.	The President's Executive Council has issued a formal request to the Department of Human Resource Development (HRD) to conduct a needs assessment.
2. Identify individuals to be involved in planning and overseeing of needs assessment.	A steering committee of six people is appointed, composed of members of the HRD Department and mid- and entry-level managers.
3. Develop focus and specific objectives for the needs assessment (answering the questions one really wants to know).	The steering committee decides to focus the needs assessment on the following two questions: (1) What are the major skills, values, attitudes, and knowledge mid-level managers need to perform effectively and efficiently in their present positions? (2) In five years, how might this list of needs change based on future forecasts and trends?
4. Determine the time frame, budget, and staff.	The steering committee determines it will need to complete the needs assessment in six months. Three members of the HRD Department will serve as staff for the project and $10,000 will be allotted for expenses.
5. Select data collection techniques.	The techniques chosen for data collection include a written survey, key informant interviews, group meetings, and a review of written materials and documents.

TABLE 6.2. Steps Involved in a Formal Needs Assessment Process (*continued*)

Steps	Example
6. Collect data.	The survey will be developed in consultation with the steering committee and administered by staff members from the HRD Department. These same staff will conduct the group sessions with selected mid-level managers and their subordinates, and review all written materials. The steering committee will conduct the key informant interviews with 12 people: two top managers, six mid-level managers, three subordinates of these managers, and one outside consultant.
7. Analyze data to determine: a. The basic findings in terms of quantitative (numerical) and qualitative descriptions, b. Points of agreement and disagreement, and c. General conclusions concerning identified needs.	An analysis of the data is completed by the HRD staff. The steering committee then reviews this analysis.
8. Further analyze the findings and conclusions to determine whether training is the best response to the needs identified.	The steering committee completes this analysis and makes its recommendations to the HRD Department.
9. Prioritize the needs identified as appropriate for a training intervention from the most to the least important using such criteria as cost, feasibility, urgency, and number of people affected.	The steering committee arrives at a consensus of which training needs should be addressed first using a priority rating instrument. This is followed by group discussions.
10. Report the results of the needs assessment to key individuals and groups within the organization.	A full report of the needs assessment process, findings, and conclusions is submitted to the President's Executive Council. An executive summary of the report is given to all mid-level managers, after the report has been approved by the Executive Council. In addition, members of the steering committee meet with key individuals from top and mid-level management to discuss preliminary ideas for training programs.

TECHNIQUES FOR DATA COLLECTION

A variety of techniques can be used in conducting a formal needs assessment. They range from highly structured and time-consuming techniques such as mail surveys, to simple observations of daily work practice. "The techniques may be used alone or in combination, depending on the objectives, the people involved, and the funding available for the needs assessment" (Caffarella, 1982, p. 8). Eight of the most widely used techniques for conducting needs assessments are covered in Table 6.3. A description of each technique is given along with a list of basic operational guidelines. The material for the table was taken from four major sources describing data collection techniques (Knowles, 1980, pp. 100-106; Steadman, 1980, p. 59; Tracey, 1984, pp. 62-71; and Zemke and Kramlinger, 1982).

TABLE 6.3. Techniques for Data Collection

Technique	Description	Operational Guidelines
Observations	Watching personnel while they work at actual or simulated job tasks.	Can be open-ended or structured with specific variables to investigate.
		Types of observations include time-motion studies, task listings, behaviorial frequency counts, and causal watching.
Surveys	Gathering opinions, attitudes, preferences, and perceptions of fact by means of a written questionnaire.	Should pretest and revise the questions and format as needed.
		Can use a variety of question formats: open-ended, ranking, checklists, forced choice.
		Can be administered through the mail or be given to individuals or groups to complete.
Interviews	Conversing with people individually or in groups, either in person or by phone.	Can be open-ended, non-directed, or formally structured, with specific questions to ask.
		Should pretest and review interview questions as needed.

TABLE 6.3. Techniques for Data Collection (continued)

Technique	Description	Operational Guidelines
Group meetings	Employees identify and analyze work-related problems in group sessions.	Start with a problem known to be of concern to group members. Use one or more group facilitating techniques: brainstorming, nominal group technique, focus group, consensus ranking, and general group discussion.
Job analysis	Process of collecting, tabulating, grouping, analyzing, interpreting, and reporting on the duties, tasks, and elements that make up a job. Identifies in precise detail: (1) the tools and conditions needed to do the job; (2) the aptitudes, skills, and knowledge required of the employee; and (3) the quantity and quality of performance required.	Be sure the analysis is of a current job and performance. Provide for data collection from all knowledgeable employees (e.g., job incumbents, supervisors, managerial personnel). Use a variety of techniques to collect data, such as questionnaires, task checklists, individual and group interviews, observations, jury of experts, work records, and analysis of technical publications.
Tests	Consists of pencil and paper or performance exercise. Used to measure an employee's knowledge, skills, or attitudes related to a specific job or job classification.	Know what the test measures (knowledge, skills, attitudes) and use as a diagnostic tool only for those areas. Choose a specific test carefully. Be sure that what the test measures is relevant and important to the particular situation in which it will be used (e.g., do not use a test for knowledge if you are really interested in skill level). Check to see if the test is both reliable and valid.

TABLE 6.3. Techniques for Data Collection (continued)

Technique	Description	Operational Guidelines
Critical incident survey	Requires employees to describe in detail an event or situation that has a significant impact on a specific job function or task.	Use only qualified observers. Incidents must represent behaviors that have direct consequences. When asking employees to describe incidents, clearly define for them: (1) the types of incidents to be recorded (e.g., successes, failures), (2) the time frame from which incidents should be chosen, and (3) that completed actions and their results should both be noted. Provide for competent leadership, and group members who are both knowledgeable and willing to participate.
Written materials	Written materials can be organizational documents or developed by outside groups. Examples of materials include: strategic planning reports, policy and procedures manuals, performance appraisal records, minutes of meetings, employee records (e.g., absenteeism, grievances, accidents), job efficiency indexes (e.g., waste, down time, repairs), monthly and annual reports, evaluation studies, reports of previous needs assessments, books, and professional and trade journal publications.	Maintain an up-to-date, active file of written materials that pertain to your training activities. Use the materials as checks, along with other techniques.

How does a person determine which technique or combination of techniques to use? Newstrom and Lilyquist (1979) developed a contingency model for selecting needs assessment techniques. They selected five criteria for differentiating among techniques:

1. Incumbent (employee) involvement
2. Management (supervisory) involvement

3. Time requirement

4. Cost

5. Relevant quantifiable data

The Newstrom and Lilyquist model (1979, p. 56), shown in Table 6.4, is used to evaluate the eight data collection techniques just presented in Table 6.3.

As seen in Table 6.4, no one technique is suitable for all situations. Each has its own strengths and weaknesses related to employee and supervisory involvement, time and budget allotments, and type of data needed. The ratings in this table can also change depending on how a needs assessment is designed and who conducts it. For example, even though administering a needs survey is usually costly and time consuming, using an already developed instrument and data analysis procedure can cut down on both expense and time.

One additional factor should be considered in choosing a needs assessment technique: the nature of the job itself. Some assessment techniques are better suited for particular jobs than others, as illustrated in Table 6.5. This evaluation of the appropriateness of various techniques for particular job classifications is not iron-clad, but generally reflects needs assessment experience.

TABLE 6.4. Evaluation of Eight Selected Needs Assessment Techniques Using the Newstrom and Lilyquist Contingency Model of Needs Assessment

Technique	Employee Involvement	Supervisory Management Involvement	Time Requirement	Cost	Relevant Quantifiable Data
Observation	Low	Moderate	Moderate	Low	Low–moderate
Survey	Moderate	Moderate	High	High	High
Interview	High	Low	High	Moderate	Moderate
Group meeting	High	Moderate	Moderate	Low	Low
Job analysis	Low	High	High	Moderate	High
Tests	Moderate	Low	Moderate	Moderate	High
Critical incident	High	High	Moderate	Low	Low
Written materials	Low	Low	Moderate	Low	Low

TABLE 6.5. Needs Assessment Techniques as Related to Job Classifications[a]

Technique	Job Classification				
	Manual	Technical	Clerical	Supervisory	Managerial
Surveys	X	X	X		
Observations				X	X
Interviews		X	X	X	X
Group meetings				X	X
Job analysis	X	X	X	X	
Tests		X	X		
Critical incident survey		X	X	X	X
Written materials		X	X	X	X

[a]X = appropriate technique for job classification.

ADDITIONAL WAYS TO GENERATE NEEDS/IDEAS FOR TRAINING ACTIVITIES

As mentioned earlier, needs and ideas for training activities are generated in a number of ways, from conducting a formal needs assessment to conversations over coffee. Some of the same techniques (e.g., observations and group meetings) used in formal needs assessments are also appropriate for gathering data in informal ways. The major difference is that these methods are then used in a less systematic way. Various techniques, along with additional ideas on ways that needs and ideas are generated, are outlined in Table 6.6.

TABLE 6.6. Additional Ways To Generate Needs/Ideas for Training Activities

How Ideas/Needs Are Generated	Description	Example
Observing employees	Watching people while they work at actual job tasks.	Joan, by observing her staff over a period of a month, notices a problem with the way most staff are responding to telephone calls from customers.

TABLE 6.6. Additional Ways To Generate Needs/Ideas for Training Activities (*continued*)

How Ideas/Needs Are Generated	Description	Example
Attending in-house group meetings	As part of regularly scheduled group meetings (e.g., weekly group staff meetings), employees identify work-related problems.	Staff from Division Y have been complaining at staff meetings over the last three weeks that they just do not understand the organization's new policy and procedures manual.
Reviewing written materials	Review of organizational documents, reports, etc., or materials developed by outside sources (e.g., performance appraisal records, minutes of meetings, reports, books, professional and trade journals).	Gail has heard through the grapevine that there appear to be problems with the way supervisors have been completing the performance appraisal reports. She decides to review a random sample of these reports to see if any specific response pattern emerges.
Responding to requests	Personnel ask that specific training activities be offered or that assistance be given in designing training programs in their particular area.	Sam, the V.P. of Operations, has requested that the HRD Department provide workshops on written communication skills for all entry-level management personnel.
Attending professional and trade meetings	Personnel involved with training attend sessions at local, regional, and national meetings that give them ideas for training activities appropriate for their organization.	Gail attends an excellent session on time management at a regional conference for personnel specialists. She believes both the content and the way the content was presented is just what her entry-level management people have been requesting in terms of an in-house workshop.

TABLE 6.6. Additional Ways To Generate Needs/Ideas for Training Activities (continued)

How Ideas/Needs Are Generated	Description	Example
Conversing with colleagues	Talking informally with colleagues both internal and external to the organization. These conversations take place over coffee, at lunch, and in the hallways.	Sue attends a local meeting of the Society for Manufacturing Engineers. Over lunch she talks with a colleague about a training program he has initiated with his organization. She's impressed and asks him to send her some material on it.
Reviewing training materials/programs	Involves gathering and analyzing training materials and programs from other organizations.	Bob has received a request to develop a series of workshops for supervisory personnel on performance appraisal. He knows of at least four other organizations in the area that have recently done this type of program. He calls the training specialist from each of these organizations and asks for copies of their programs so he can review them for possible adoption.

DETERMINING WHETHER TRAINING IS AN APPROPRIATE RESPONSE TO NEEDS/PROBLEMS/IDEAS

Developing training activities is not the only or best way to meet various ideas and needs that have been identified. Thus one of the final steps in needs analysis is determining whether training is the best answer to the problems and needs presented and, if not, what other alternatives might be better. A process for doing this is outlined:

Give a description of the need/problem/idea identified, using the information gathered during the idea generating stage. Be as detailed as possible in this description.

Determine whether the need/problem/idea that has been identified is performance-related. Although some training activities are designed around nonjob-related issues, most are not. It is important to determine this upfront. Answering two questions will help in making this judgment: (1) Does the need/problem/idea describe what employees are presently doing that they should not be doing? (2) Does it define what they are not doing that they should be doing? (Laird, 1985). If the answer to question 2 is that the need/problem/idea identified is performance-related, then go on to the next step. If not, then an alternative to training is probably a better solution.

Classify the need/problem/idea as something that employees: (1) do not know (lack of knowledge), (2) cannot do (lack of skill), or (3) can do, but do not care to do (lack of motivation) (Knowles, 1980; Laird, 1985; Michalak and Yager, 1979). If the need/problem/idea has been classified as a lack of knowledge or skill, then training is probably indicated. If it has been classified as a lack of motivation, then an alternative solution is usually required.

A number of alternatives to training have been proposed by different authors (Gane, 1972; Michalak and Yager, 1979; Laird, 1985; Nadler, 1982; Warren, 1979). These are outlined in Table 6.7 according to three major categories: (1) individual, (2) job specific, and (3) organizational.

TABLE 6.7. Alternatives to Training

Alternatives for Individuals	Job Specific Alternatives	Organizational Alternatives
Provide job aids (e.g., checklists, charts, memory joggers, reference aids)	Redefine the job	Improve selection methods and criteria for hiring
Transfer or terminate the individual	Change the equipment	Change the reward structure (e.g., contingencies, benefits, salary)
	Change the conditions under which the job is performed (e.g., lighting, cooling)	Change the organizational structure and/or support patterns (e.g., have unit report to different group within the organization)
	Change the performance standards	
	Communicate the performance standards differently	
	Eliminate the job	

The most frequently used alternatives to training are individually oriented or job specific. For example, job aids are standard items for many organizations. Examples of such aids are flowcharts on how to start up and shut down a piece of equipment, or lists of personnel with their office numbers and extensions. Job redesign has been another popular response to organizational problems or needs. Often job redesign and the introduction of new equipment go hand-in-hand. Having employees use computers as a normal part of their work is an excellent example of this.

SUMMARY

1. An educational need is usually defined as a discrepancy or gap between what presently is and what should be. It may be a gap in desired versus actual productivity, a discrepancy between what a supervisor wants staff to do and how they actually perform, or employees' perception of a lack of knowledge or skill in contrast to what they believe they should know or be able to do.

2. Training needs are generated from three primary sources: people, the job, and the organization. Often the first sign that training might be needed surfaces as a specific problem. At this point, the job of the trainer is to define the problem in more depth. Is the problem performance-related? Is it a new or recurring problem and how many employees does it affect?

3. There are many ways to generate ideas and needs for training programs. One major way is by conducting a formal needs assessment. Alternative ways include conversing with colleagues, reviewing vendor training programs, and attending professional and trade meetings.

4. A formal needs assessment is a systematic way to identify educational deficiencies or problems. One model, consisting of 10 steps for completing this process, is:
   a. Make a conscious decision to complete a needs assessment process with a commitment to planning
   b. Identify individuals to be involved in planning and overseeing the needs assessment
   c. Develop the focus and specific objectives for the needs assessment
   d. Determine the time frame, budget, and staff
   e. Select data collection techniques
   f. Collect data

g. Analyze data

h. Further analyze the findings and conclusions to determine whether training is the best response

i. Prioritize the needs identified as appropriate for a training intervention

j. Report the results to key individuals and groups within the organization

5. A variety of techniques can be used in conducting a formal needs assessment. Eight of the most widely used techniques include: observations, surveys, interviews, group meetings, job analyses, tests, critical incident surveys, and written materials.

6. No one technique is suitable for gathering needs assessment data. Each has its own strengths and weaknesses related to the employee level and supervisory involvement desired, time and budget allocations, type of data needed, and the nature of the job itself.

7. Developing training activities is not the only or best way to meet various needs and ideas that have been identified. Thus a final step in needs analysis is determining whether training is the best answer to the problems and needs presented and, if not, what other alternatives might be better.

1. Outline on the following chart what your sources of training needs/ideas are in your role as a training specialist. Be as specific as possible in naming those sources, including such items as names of individuals and groups, titles of reports and documents, and where the sources can be located.

Sources	Internal to Organization	External to Organization
People **individuals** **groups**		
Job **specific**		
Organization		

2. Based on the material you outlined in the chart, make a list of those sources that you would use first, second, and third. Are there any you would choose not to use at this time?

Sources you would use first: _____

_____

_____

_____

Sources you would use second: _____

_____

_____

_____

Sources you would use third: _____

_____

_____

_____

Sources you would not choose to use at this time: _____

_____

_____

_____

_____

1. Identify a job-related problem (e.g., poor communication, low productivity, frequent absenteeism) for which you believe a training program would be appropriate.

_____

_____

_____

_____

2. Think about doing a formal needs assessment related to the problem you identified and decide, using the following chart, whether there is a low, moderate, or high need for each of the five factors given. Check each box that applies.

			Criteria		
Level	**Need for Employees to Be Involved**	**Need for Supervisors to Be Involved**	**Time Allotted**	**Budget Allotted**	**Need for Quantifiable Data**
High					
Moderate					
Low					

3. Is the job a manual, clerical, technical, supervisory, or managerial position?

_____

_____

4. Using the materials in Table 6.4 (Evaluation of Eight Selected Needs Assessment Techniques Using the Newstrom and Lilyquist Contingency Model of Needs Assessment) and Table 6.5 (Needs Assessment Techniques as Related to Job Classifications), choose at least two assessment techniques that would be appropriate for the situation presented.

a. _____

_____

b. _____

_____

▶CHAPTER 6, WORKSHEET 3: DETERMINING WHETHER TRAINING IS APPROPRIATE

1. Outline a problem or need in your organization for which you believe a training activity might be a good reponse. Be as specific as possible.

_____

_____

_____

_____

2. Determine whether the need or problem you have identified is performance-related and why or why not. If it is performance-related, go on to number 3. If it is not performance-related, go to number 4 of this worksheet.

_____

_____

_____

_____

3. Classify the need or problem you have identified as something your employees: (check as appropriate)

   a. Do not know (lack of knowledge) _____
   b. Cannot do (lack of skill) _____
   c. Can do, but do not care to do (lack of motivation) _____

If it is a lack of skill or knowledge, then a training activity is an appropriate solution. If you have classified it as a lack of motiviation, go to number 4 of this worksheet.

4. Identify possible alternative solutions (other than training) to the problem or need you have identified. List these alternatives.

_____

_____

_____

_____

_____

_____

7

DETERMINING PRIORITIES FOR TRAINING

Rarely can personnel involved with training respond to all of the needs and ideas identified as appropriate for training. Thus they must have a system for determining which ideas and needs will take priority in planning actual training events.

DEFINING PRIORITIES

What constitutes a priority need or idea? A priority is often thought of as the most important or most urgent need to be addressed. Depending on the situation, however, other factors must be considered, such as the number of people affected and availability of resources. As Sork states:

> *What is being done in determining priorities is to assign preferential ratings to needs which are in competition for available resources so that judgments can be made about how those resources will be allocated.*
>
> (SORK, 1982, P. 1)

WHY SET PRIORITIES?

Why do training personnel need to set priorities? Forest and Mulcahy (1976), as presented in Table 7.1, have outlined five major reasons for doing priority setting as a normal part of program planning. Some of the reasons are important to the clientele and the organization, while others are important to the training personnel themselves.

TABLE 7.1. Why Set Priorities?

Reason for Setting Priorities	Of Primary Importance	Example from the Work Setting
To meet the changing needs and roles of employers	Clientele and organization	By the second quarter all supervisory personnel are expected to do their record keeping on desk-top computers.
To prevent crisis situations	Organization	Through prioritizing, training specialists discovered why productivity was down on machine 1: the employees were operating the machine incorrectly and in a very unsafe manner.
To enhance credibility and accountability	Training personnel	A special training report was routed through the president's office and, as a result, the training department was commended by the CEO.
To make the job easier	Training personnel	The training staff now have a clear picture of what types of activities need to be scheduled over the next year.
To help allocate and coordinate resources	Organization and training personnel	Priorities 1 to 3 will receive 50% of the allotted resources. Other needs will be met as resources allow.

WHO SETS PRIORITIES?

Who should be involved in setting priorities? Depending on the situation, any combination of the following people may be appropriate:

1. Staff involved with training
2. Potential participants

3. Supervisors of potential participants

4. Key management personnel

5. Personnel from outside the organization (e.g., consumers, community leaders, consultants) (Boyle, 1981; Forest and Mulcahy, 1976; Kaufman and Stone, 1983).

Training personnel may consult with these people on an individual basis and/or involve them in group discussions. Group meetings may be of an informal nature or they may be formally organized committees, such as the training committee.

For example, John A., director of management development, might first talk informally with individual key managers in the organization concerning a report he has prepared on the major training needs of entry-level managers. He might then ask a group of entry-level managers and their supervisors to form an ad hoc committee to review the material and develop priorities for training activities based on the same report. His final step might be to have the training committee, using the priorities generated by both key management personnel and the ad hoc committee, make the final recommendations on what specific training programs should be offered for entry-level managers.

DEVELOPING ASSUMPTIONS ON WHICH TO BASE PRIORITY DECISIONS

Prior to initiating the priority setting process, it is important to develop a set of assumptions as a context within which the decisions will be made. Five major categories of influence need to be considered in developing these assumptions, drawn primarily from the work of Boyle (1981) and Forest and Mulcahy (1976). These categories include situational variables, organizational variables, potential participants, personnel, and resources.

Situational Variables

In making priority decisions, training personnel must have a clear understanding of both the new ideas and needs that have been identified and of present training priorities and commitments. These commitments may include carry-over programs and activities that must be repeated.

Interpreting ideas and needs in terms of present activities can be handled in three ways. The first is to consider the present commitments as possible priorities, "along with other emerging and new concerns. Selecting this option means some present commitments eventually will be rated a lower priority" (Forest and Mulcahy, 1976, p. 17). A second approach is to recognize that prior or ongoing commitments will take time and therefore time must be set aside to meet them. Third, the past priorities and commitments can be ignored. Realistically, this alternative will not be very popular because commitments are often made to get or keep the support of others. "Regardless of the approach, all traditional, repetitious, and ongoing activities and commitments, as well as emerging concerns, must be considered when setting new priorities" (Forest and Mulcahy, 1976, p. 17).

Situational Variables: Sample Assumption

All present commitments, along with new ideas and concerns, will be considered as possible priorities on an equal basis.

Organizational Variables

Decisions about priorities are made in light of the organization's mission and goals. For example: Does the organization expect that training activities will result in greater productivity and thus cost savings? Is it expected that training should itself be a profit-making operation? Will innovative training programs be supported or only those that have stood the test of time? Is the organization primarily interested in technical training or is the "broader" type of training (e.g., communication skills, time management) equally acceptable?

In addition, it is necessary to consider the politics of the organization. How are decisions made and who makes them? Are there power coalitions, both formal and informal, that training personnel need to cultivate? How can training staff wisely use the political structure to enhance their programs? "The question—'Is it politically feasible?'—is always relevant" (Boyle, 1981, pp. 174).

Organizational Variables: Sample Assumption

Is it expected that training will result in increased productivity of employees? This must be demonstrated through a cost-benefit analysis.

Potential Participants

It is important at the start to have a clear picture of who are the potential participants. One way of doing this is to do a target population analysis. Eight important questions need to be asked to complete this analysis:

1. How many people might be involved?
2. At what times might the potential participants be able to come to training?
3. Where are the potential participants located in the organization?
4. What are the ages of the potential participants?
5. What are the educational levels of the potential participants?
6. What can be assumed about the present and past job experiences of the potential participants?
7. What are the potential participants' motivation for training?
8. What are the costs (real dollars, loss of time on job) to the potential participants for attending the program? (Gane, 1972; Strother and Klus, 1982)

Training personnel also should have a clear understanding of the needs and interests of the potential participants from the perspective of those participants. Scissons (1982) has stressed that employee needs should be examined in terms of three components: competence, relevance, and motivation. Competence is defined as the individual's self-appraisal of his or her ability to perform a wide range of tasks. Relevance is the individual's self-assessment of the importance of the task to his or her specific situation. Motivation is the individual's stated willingness to engage in a training activity for self-improvement. In determining priorities, the ideal situation is to list items that individual employees have rated high in relevance and motivation.

Potential Participants: Sample Assumption

The participants for the program will include all entry- and mid-level managers. They are all college educated and are located in 25 different locations across the state. Their ages range from 23 to 45.

Personnel

Staff members use their own values, perceptions, and experiences in making priority decisions about which needs or ideas should be responded to first. Thus it is important to know who the personnel are who will be involved in making these decisions. What are their educational backgrounds? What kinds of work experience have they had? Are they more oriented toward a bottom-line perspective or toward the growth and development of employees? What are their perceptions of the whole training enterprise?

The influence of training personnel as educational leaders within the organization is important, but it should not take precedence over the opinions and experiences of other types of staff. In the final analysis, whatever priorities are selected, they must become the personal priorities of the training staff because they are responsible for getting the job done.

Personnel: Sample Assumption

A team of three people, composed of two training specialists and their supervisor, will determine the priorities for training for the next six months.

Resources

In determining priorities, the types and amounts of resources available for training must be spelled out. Resources include time, money, personnel, facilities, equipment, material, and supplies. Boyle has outlined three key questions that need to be answered about resources in setting priorities: "Do we have the quality and quantity of resources necessary to affect change through a program? Are they the right kind of resources? Are we employing new personnel to coincide with changing program priorities?" (Boyle, 1981, p. 174).

Resources: Sample Assumption

No new financial resources will be available to the training department. The department may choose to reallocate present resources, including staff time and funds available for programs.

HOW ARE PRIORITIES SET?

Determining priorities is a dynamic process of deciding which needs or ideas are most important now, and making a commitment of self and resources to that decision (Forest and Mulcahy, 1976). Importance is defined primarily in terms of value and time. It is deciding what needs doing first, what needs doing most, and how much time to give it. This decision-making process can be done in either a haphazard or a systematic way. The more systematic the priority setting process, the greater likelihood that training activities will reflect the primary needs and ideas of the potential participants and of the organization as a whole. The following two scenarios illustrate this proposition.

SCENARIO ONE. Ellen has just been appointed as the Director of Training for the Marketing and Sales Division. She has been a top salesperson herself as well as a District Sales Manager. Because the position has been vacant for six months, there is a pile of requests for training programs sitting on her desk. In addition, her predecessor had conducted an organizational wide needs assessment for the division, but none of the recommendations have yet been implemented. Ellen decides she should get some programs up and running fast. She first chooses a set of "canned programs" on time management because the sales staff from her old district really had problems in that area and she remembers that it was mentioned somewhere in the needs assessment report. In addition, Ellen responds to three of the many requests she has on her desk. It just so happens that these three requests are from colleagues whom she knows she can count on to get people to the programs. Ellen believes she is in good shape because she now has programs scheduled for at least the next three months.

SCENARIO TWO. Brian has just been asked to develop a series of training programs for all nursing staff in the hospital. The previous Director of Staff Development had conducted an extensive organizational wide needs analysis of nursing personnel. In addition, a number of head nurses have requested different types of programs for their staff. Brian believes he must initiate some activities quickly. He decides to respond first to those requests made by the head nurses, and then to the more comprehensive recommendations from the needs assessment. He asks the director of nursing and three head nurses to assist him in determining which requests should be handled first. To help them, he identifies three major criteria on which the judgments should be made: (1) number of people affected, (2) immediacy of the need presented, and (3) apparent commitment of the nursing staff to attend such a program. Once this process is complete and programs are planned, Brian then plans to form an ad hoc planning committee to determine program priorities for the next one to two years.

A SYSTEMATIC PROCESS
FOR DETERMINING PRIORITIES

Based primarily on the work of Sork (1979, 1982), a five-step process is described for systematically determining priorities among identified needs and ideas. The key element is establishing early in the process clear criteria for analyzing the data and converting it into priorities.

STEP ONE. Identify the people who should be involved in setting priorities.

As mentioned earlier in this chapter, a number of different types of personnel are appropriate for doing priority setting, from potential participants to key management personnel, depending on the situation. "Included should be those who are in a position to allocate resources and who are interested in employing a systematic procedure for determining priorities" (Sork, 1982, p. 9).

STEP TWO. Prepare a set of assumptions on which the decisions will be made.

These assumptions, described on pages 000–000, should address specific situational and organizational variables, potential participants, personnel, and the types and amounts of resources available. Completing this step provides the foundation for step three, which is the selection of criteria on which priority decisions will be made.

STEP THREE. Select or develop appropriate criteria.

As noted earlier, selecting criteria is the key element in determining priorities. These criteria provide not only the basis on which priorities are made, but also serve as the justification for the eventual choices. "No one criterion or set of criteria fits all situations and there are no formulas or guidelines for selecting criteria" (Sork, 1982, p. 2).

Kaufman and Stone (1983) have suggested two different criteria systems based on specified categories. One set of categories is (Kaufman and Stone, 1983, p. 94):

Critical (must be resolved in the next six months)

Very important (must be resolved in the next year)

Important (should be resolved within two years)

Minimal (should be dealt with, but only if enough time and resources are left over from higher priority needs)

Not important (not necessary to deal with)

Not a need

Another "sort" might be:

Highest 5 percent of all needs

Highest 20 percent of all needs

Middle 50 percent of all needs

Lowest 20 percent of all needs

Lowest 5 percent of all needs

Sork (1982) has approached criteria development in a somewhat different way. He has suggested that criteria generally fall into two major categories: importance and feasibility. An overall judgment about a need or idea could be made by rating needs only on their relative importance and/or their relative feasibility. He then elaborates further by adding specific criteria for each category. Sork's eight examples of more specific criteria are outlined in Table 7.2.

TABLE 7.2. Sork's Suggested Criteria for Determining Priorities

Criteria	Description
Importance Criteria	
Number of people affected	An estimate of how many people would be involved if a specific need were addressed.
Contribution to goals	The degree to which meeting the need would contribute to the attainment of organizational goals.
Immediacy	The degree to which each need requires immediate attention.
Instrumental value	The degree to which one need will have a positive or negative effect on meeting other needs.
Magnitude of discrepancy	The relative size of the gap (measurable discrepancy) between the present state of affairs and a more desirable future state of affairs.
Feasibility Criteria	
Educational efficacy	The degree to which a training intervention (program or series of programs) can contribute to eliminating the need.
Availability of resources	The degree to which the resources necessary to meet the need would be available if it is decided that the need should be addressed (e.g., personnel, financial, equipment, facilities).
Commitment to change	The degree to which those with vested interests (e.g., participants, supervisors, top management) are committed to eliminating the need. This commitment may be positive or negative.

SOURCE: Sork, Thomas J. *Determining Priorities*. Vancouver: British Columbia Ministry of Education, 1982, pp. 2–4. Reprinted with permission.

Sork explains that these eight criteria are only one set of choices on which decisions about priorities can be made. Other criteria might be more appropriate, depending on the mission and goals of the organization.

STEP FOUR. Record the needs or ideas, along with the criteria, on a priority rating chart. Assign, where appropriate, weighting factors to each criterion.

It is helpful to develop priority rating charts, especially when priorities are determined by a number of individuals. The charts can be completed individually and then the ratings compared, or they may be completed by a group as a whole. The size and complexity of the chart depends on: (1) how many criteria have been chosen, and (2) whether all the criteria should be rated equally or whether some criteria should have greater impact than others on the decision. A sample of a priority chart where all criteria are weighted equally is given in Table 7.3.

When the decision makers believe that some of the criteria should have more impact on the decision than others, weighting factors need to be assigned to each criteria.

> One straightforward way to carry out this task is to first identify the criterion which should carry the least weight in priority decisions. This criterion is assigned a weighting factor of "1." All other criteria are then assigned weighting factors based on the desired weight they should carry in relation to the first criterion.
>
> (SORK, 1982, P. 5)

Sork (1982) has developed a sample priority chart in which different weights are given to different criteria, as shown in Table 7.4.

TABLE 7.3. Priority Chart: All Criteria Weighted Equally

Items To Be Prioritized	Number of People Affected	Contribution To Goals	Immediacy	Availability of Resources

TABLE 7.4. Priority Ranking Chart: Criteria Weighted Differently

Needs/Ideas	Criteria					Sum of Weighted Ranks	Mean Weighted Rank	Final Rank
	Wt. = ___	Wt. = ___	Wt. = ___	Wt. = ___	Wt. = ___			

SOURCE: Sork, Thomas J. *Determining Priorities*. Vancouver: British Columbia Ministry of Education, 1982, p. 8. Reprinted with permission.

STEP FIVE. Apply each criterion to each need using the priority rating chart. Combine individual values to yield a total priority value for each need, where appropriate.

When applying criteria that are weighted equally, two alternative systems are suggested. The first is to do a simple ranking of each item on each criterion from "1" (highest) to "N" (lowest). The rankings are then totaled and the one receiving the lowest number will be considered the top priority. An example of this system is pictured in Table 7.5. The top priority in this example would be assigning work to employees, with communication a close second.

An alternative way to assign priorities when criteria are equally weighted is to assign each item a rating such as high, medium, and low (see Table 7.6). The results of this can then be discussed for points of agreement and disagreement, again with top priority given to those items receiving the highest ratings. It is important to specify what the ratings mean prior to completing the chart.

TABLE 7.5. Example of Priority Rating Chart: Criteria Are Rated Equally

Items to Be Prioritized: Needs of Supervisor	Number of People Affected	Contribution To Goals	Immediacy	Availability of Resources	Total Score
Assigning work to employees	1	1	3	1	6
Communicating effectively (oral and written)	2	3	1	3	9
Counseling on attendance, performance, and work habits	4	4	2	5	15
Dealing with conflict situations	5	5	5	2	17
Motivating employees	3	2	4	4	13

TABLE 7.6. Example of Priority Rating Chart: Using High, Medium, and Low

Items to Be Prioritized: Needs of Supervisors	Number of People Affected	Contribution To Goals	Immediacy	Availability of Resources	Overall Rating
Assigning work to employees	Low	High	High	High	High
Communicating effectively (oral and written)	High	Medium	Low	Medium	Medium
Counseling on attendance, performance and work habits	Medium	High	High	Low	Medium
Dealing with conflict situations	Low	Low	Low	Medium	Low
Motivating employees	Medium	Medium	High	High	Medium/ High

In using a priority system in which the criteria are not equally weighted, the process is more complex. Sork has suggested one way for completing this process:

1. For each criterion rank all needs from "1" (representing the highest priority) to "N" (representing the lowest priority).
2. Multiply the rankings by the weighting factors.
3. Add the weighted ranks for each need (across the rows) and record the sum in the "Sum of Weighted Ranks" column.
4. Divide the sum of ranks by the number of criteria and record the result in the "Mean Weighted Rank" column.
5. Assign a final rank to each need based on the "Mean Weighted Rank" with the lowest score receiving a priority of "1" and the highest a priority of "N."

(SORK, 1982, PP. 10–11.)

An example of a completed chart using this system can be seen in Table 7.7. Again Sork emphasizes that his suggested procedure is only one alternative for determining priorities when the criteria are not equally weighted.

TABLE 7.7. Example of Priority Ranking Chart: Criteria Weighted Differently

	Criteria						
Needs/Ideas	Number of People Affected Wt. = 2	Contribution to Goals Wt. = 7	Immediacy Wt. = 5	Availability of Resources Wt. = 9	Sum of Weighted Ranks	Mean Weighted Rank	Final Rank
Assigning work to employees	1 2	1 7	3 15	1 9	33	6.6	1
Communicating effectively (oral and written)	2 4	3 21	1 5	3 27	57	11.5	2
Counseling on attendance, performance, and work habits	4 8	4 28	2 10	5 45	91	18.2	5
Dealing with conflict situations	5 10	5 35	5 25	2 18	88	17.6	4
Motivating employees	3 6	2 14	4 20	4 36	76	15.5	3

MAKING A COMMITMENT TO ACT ON THE PRIORITIES

Making a commitment to act means mapping out just how the ideas/needs chosen as priorities will be addressed. One way to do this is to develop a master schedule that outlines what has to be done, by whom, and when. Table 7.8 is an example of a master schedule for an entry-level management training program.

This master plan should serve as a guide to subsequent actions, but by no means should it be seen as "set in stone." It can also be a powerful motivator for getting the job done. This is especially true if the plan has been reviewed by personnel in the organization who are relying on the training staff to respond to their needs and ideas in a timely manner.

TABLE 7.8. Master Plan for Acting on Procedures

Needs/Ideas Identified As Priorities	Actions To Be Taken	Personnel Responsible for Actions	Resources Needed	Target Date
Communication skills	Develop a one-day workshop	Judy O., Training Specialist	Unit on communications skills Instructional materials and handouts	Oct. 1
Conducting performance appraisals	Develop a two-day workshop followed by supervisor coaching	Bob Q., Training Specialist, plus three mid-level managers	Company information packet on performance appraisal Resource manual Instructional materials	Nov. 15
Using your desk-top computer effectively	Develop a course that meets once per week for an eight-week period	Sue P., Training Specialist and outside consultant	A new curriculum package for this course	Jan. 15

SUMMARY

1. Rarely can personnel involved with training respond to all the needs and ideas identified as appropriate for training. Thus they must have a system for determining which needs and ideas will take priority in planning actual training events.

2. A priority is often thought of as the most important or the most urgent need to be addressed. Depending on the situation, however, other factors must be considered, such as the number of people affected and the availability of resources.

3. Training personnel need to set priorities for five major reasons:
   a. To meet the changing needs and roles of employers
   b. To prevent crisis situations
   c. To enhance credibility and accountability
   d. To make the job easier
   e. To help allocate and coordinate resources

4. Any combination of the following people may be appropriate to assist in setting priorities for training: training staff, potential participants, supervisors of potential participants, key management personnel, and personnel from outside the organization. Training personnel may consult with these people on an individual basis and/or involve them in group discussions.

5. Prior to initiating the priority setting process, it is important to develop a set of assumptions as a context within which decisions will be made. Five major categories of influence—situational variables, organizational variables, potential participants, personnel, and resources—need to be considered in developing these assumptions.

6. Determining priorities is a dynamic process of deciding which needs or ideas are important now and making a commitment of self and others to that decision. A five- step process for systematically determining priorities is outlined:

   STEP ONE. Identify the people who should be involved in setting priorities.

   STEP TWO. Prepare a set of assumptions on which the decision will be made.

   STEP THREE. Select or develop appropriate criteria.

   STEP FOUR. Record the needs or ideas, along with the criteria, on a priority rating chart. Assign weighting factors to each criterion, where appropriate.

STEP FIVE. Apply each criterion to each need using the priority rating chart. Combine individual values to yield a total priority value for each need, where appropriate.

7. The key element in the priority setting process is establishing clear criteria for analyzing the data and converting it into priorities. The criteria provide not only the basis on which priorities are made, but also serve as the justification for the eventual choices. No one criterion or set of criteria fits all situations.

8. Making a commitment to act on priorities means mapping out on a master schedule how the ideas/needs chosen as priorities will be addressed. This master plan should serve as a guide to subsequent actions, but by no means should it be seen as "set in stone."

▶ CHAPTER 7, WORKSHEET 1: DEVELOPING ASSUMPTIONS

1. Briefly outline a situation in which you have the responsibility for developing training program priorities.

_____

_____

_____

_____

2. In the following five categories list the assumptions you need to make before you initiate your priority setting process. Be as specific as you can.

Situational Variables: _____

_____

Organizational Variables: _____

_____

Potential participants: _____

_____

Personnel: _____

_____

Resources: _____

_____

▶ CHAPTER 7, WORKSHEET 2: SETTING THE PRIORITIES

Using the instructions given here, complete the following priority rating chart.

1. List 5 to 10 needs or ideas identified by your organization as appropriate for training activities.

2. Select appropriate criteria on which those activities should be judged.

3. Assign weighting factors to each of the criterion.

4. Rank each criterion for all needs from "1" (representing the highest priority to) "N" (representing the lowest priority).

5. Multiply the rankings by the weighting factors.

6. Add the weighted ranks for each need (across the rows) and record the sum in the "Sum of Weighted Ranks" column.

7. Divide the sum of ranks by the number of criteria and record the result in the "Mean Weighted Rank" column.

8. Assign a final rank to each need based on the "Mean Weighted Rank," with the lowest score receiving a priority of "1" and the highest a priority of "N" (Instructions 3–7 are taken from Sork, 1982, pp. 10–11).

Priority Ranking Chart: Criteria Weighted Differently

Needs/Ideas	Criteria				Sum of Weighted Ranks	Mean Weighted Rank	Final Rank
	Wt. = __	Wt. = __	Wt. = __	Wt. = __			

Source: Sork, Thomas J. *Determining Priorities.* Vancouver: British Columbia Ministry of Education, 1982, p. 8. Reprinted with permission.

►CHAPTER 7, WORKSHEET 3:
DEVELOPING A MASTER PLAN

Using the instructions given here, complete the following master plan chart.

1. List three needs or ideas that have been identified by your organization as priorities around which training activities should be developed.

2. Determine the appropriate actions to be taken and the personnel who will be responsible for those actions.

3. Outline the resources that will be needed and the projected date the training activities will be held.

Needs/ Ideas	Actions To Be Taken	Personnel Responsible	Resources Needed	Target Date
1.				
2.				
3.				

8

IDENTIFYING PROGRAM OBJECTIVES

Often personnel involved with training ask themselves the question: What is the best way to let others in the organization know what we are doing? Sam R., Director of the Management Development Training Program, has thought about this question many times and especially now as his organization is going through a cost-reduction phase. Although the Management Development Training Program has an excellent reputation among the management personnel, there are those located in the technical side of the organization that view the program as just "fun and games." Sam does have a two-page information sheet that he sends out bimonthly and the annual report, which he sends to all mid- and upper-level managers. Still, the information somehow seems fragmented in describing what he believes to be the essence of his program activities: to increase the productivity of management personnel primarily through knowledge and skill building. He has often thought that if he could develop a set of objectives describing the proposed results of the management development program it could be a very useful information and planning tool. Perhaps these objectives could be similar to the objectives his own staff develop as part of the organization's Management By Objectives (MBO) Program. He could then distribute these program objectives to key personnel at the start of each calendar year and perhaps use them as the basis for writing his annual report.

WHAT ARE PROGRAM OBJECTIVES?

Program objectives are statements of what is to be achieved by the training function. They provide concrete guidelines for program development and give both focus and direction to the program. They also serve as benchmarks against which the training function can be evaluated (Knowles, 1980). Program objectives differ from instructional objectives in that instructional objectives refer to a particular learning activity, while program objectives cover a much broader range of training activities.

For example, in developing a national conference, the national conference committee would develop a broad set of program goals and objectives for the conference as a whole, based on the general theme of the conference. These would be listed in brochures describing the conference. In addition, each conference presenter would develop instructional objectives for his or her session, outlining specifically what the participants would know or be able to do as a result of that session.

This same theme of broad (program objectives) versus specific (learning objectives) can be applied to training programs within an organization. For example, Kathy W. has the responsibility for overseeing all of the technical skills training programs for Division Y. She develops, with the assistance of her staff, a set of program objectives for the 1987-1988 budget year. A sample of these objectives is:

1. To provide a series of training programs on equipment operation and safety for all line personnel

2. To institute a training program on quality circles for all line supervisors

3. To develop a series of training packages on plant safety that can be distributed to all subsidiary operations of the organization

4. To locate and equip five additional rooms for small group training for technical personnel

In addition, Kathy requires her staff to develop learning objectives for each of the training sessions and classes they coordinate. It is Kathy's job to ensure that what is happening in each of the individual training sessions does in fact meet the technical training department's program objectives. A more detailed overview of instructional objectives is given in Chapter 11.

Why are program objectives needed? Giegold and Grindle (1983) have outlined three major purposes for developing program objectives: (1) to document clearly where you are going, (2) to facilitate measuring progress and achievement, and (3) to increase motivation to get the job done. For program objectives to be useful, these authors feel that each objective should address all three purposes.

FOCUS OF PROGRAM OBJECTIVES

Program objectives describe expected or desired changes in the intended participants as a group or changes in the organization (Boyle, 1981). Changes in the participants identify what they will learn and how their job performances should change. Changes in the organization relate to the maintenance and improvement of the training function itself and how training will benefit subsections of the organization or the organization as a whole. It is important to include both types of program objectives, as appropriate. Those objectives directed at the training function itself and the overall organization are often overlooked. Examples of program objectives focused on the participants and the organization are given in Table 8.1.

TABLE 8.1. Examples of Program Objectives

Focus	Program Objectives
Participants' learning	To provide a training program on oral and written communications skills for all supervisory level 1 and 2 personnel.
Change in job performance	To reduce by 50% the number of personnel who are absent in a month's time period for Divisions X and Y.
Organization training function	To provide more adequate physical facilities for training. This will include the refurbishing of three training rooms and remodeling of an additional 500 square feet of space into an individualized instructional lab.
Organization as a whole	To institute a quality circles program for all management-level personnel.

FORM OF PROGRAM OBJECTIVES

It has been said that good program objectives must be stated in measurable terms. Although it is helpful to have them written this way, it is not always possible or preferable. "Decisions about the form of written objectives must reflect a variety of factors, including the learner, the organization, the material to be learned and the extent of . . . change being sought" (Nadler, 1982, p. 106).

For example, it is fairly easy to develop measurable objectives for training programs on skill building or knowledge acquisition. It is more difficult to develop such objectives when the program's overall objective is to enhance the creativity, confidence, or sensitivity of the participants. In these latter instances, program objectives would be directed more toward the personal growth of participants and not to a measurable end product, such as a specific behavioral change.

107

Mehrens and Lehmann (1978) agree that most educational programs have outcomes that are both measurable and not measurable. They stress also the idea of intended and unanticipated outcomes, because it is almost impossible to know beforehand all the benefits a program could produce. Thus, in defining program objectives, it is important to state both measurable and immeasurable objectives, and to leave those objectives somewhat open ended so that unanticipated but important achievements of the program can be noted. This notion of measurable and immeasurable and intended and unanticipated accomplishments is outlined in Table 8.2, with examples of specific program objectives and statements given.

Although Mehrens and Lehmann make the point that there will always be unanticipated and immeasurable outcomes, they stress the idea that these types should be few in number.

In summary, the most important things about the form of program objectives are that they: (1) have meaning for the training staff, potential participants, top management, and other key organizational personnel, and (2) provide direction and guidance for the program.

TABLE 8.2. Examples of Intended and Unanticipated Achievements, Which Are Either Measurable or Immeasurable

	Intended Achievements Stated Prior to the Program Being Carried Out	*Unanticipated Achievements* Stated During or After Program Has Been Carried Out
Measurable Achievements	To provide a training program on time management for all entry-level managers. As a result of the program, the managers will be able to demonstrate at least two ways they have restructured their day to save at least one hour of time per week. This must be verified by each manager's supervisor.	About 25% of the secretaries for the entry-level managers told their bosses that it took them less time now to manage their calendars and monitor their telephone calls.
Immeasurable Achievements	To assist entry-level managers to take more control over their daily work lives.	A number of the entry-level managers remarked on the evaluation that they felt more confident to carry out their jobs.

SOURCE: Adapted from *Measurement and Evaluation in Education and Psychology*, 2e, William Mehrens and Irvin J. Lehmann. Copyright © 1973 by Holt, Rinehart and Winston, Inc. Copyright © 1978 by Holt, Rinehart and Winston, p. 46. Reprinted by permission of Holt, Rinehart and Winston, Inc.

GUIDELINES FOR WRITING GOOD PROGRAM OBJECTIVES

When developing program objectives, training personnel should start with the needs and ideas identified as priorities for training (Nadler, 1982). These priority statements provide the base on which program objectives are formulated for groups of participants and perhaps for the organization as a whole. In addition, training personnel should define program objectives directed at maintaining and improving the training function itself. Although this latter type of program objective is probably more applicable to formal training units, these types of objectives may also prove useful to personnel who conduct training activities as part of their other job responsibilities. For example, a head nurse responsible for the in-service training of her staff may note that she does not have adequate audiovisual equipment. Thus she may define as one of her program objectives to locate and secure by April 1, the following audiovisual equipment: an overhead projector, a carousel slide projector, a videotape player and monitor, and a hanging screen.

"Training personnel should never determine program objectives in a vacuum. It is relatively easy to sit at one's desk, carefully writing objectives, but there is always the risk of producing irrelevant statements" (Nadler, 1982, p. 108). Rather, other personnel should be asked to help in developing objectives. This can be done in a number of ways. For example, training staff could request key supervisors of potential participants to help draft and/or review program objectives for their people. They could also ask a sample of potential participants to do this same process. Questions and comments from both these groups could be elicited on the relevance and usefulness of the objectives and whether or not they are understandable, especially concerning actual job practice.

Program objectives "should be stated clearly enough to indicate to all rational minds exactly what is intended." (Houle, 1972, p. 149) If a formal training committee exists, this committee could serve as a review board and give advice and counsel in the initial writing and/or redrafting of the objectives. Boyle (1981) has prepared a set of guidelines that may be helpful to personnel in developing objectives. Not all of the guidelines outlined in Table 8.3 are necessarily applicable to every objective developed.

Boyle stresses that the wording used must be applicable to the specific programming situation and must clearly communicate the proposed accomplishments of the program. As discussed earlier in this chapter, the exact form of the program objectives "is not as important as is whether the objectives are meaningful and used" (Boyle, 1981, p. 201).

TABLE 8.3. Guidelines for Stating Program Objectives

Specifies the type of participant who is expected to secure results.

Indicates the minimum number or proportion of the target clientele that are expected to show results.

Indicates what the participants are expected to achieve through the program.

Deals with things important and valuable to the prospective clientele.

Shows a clear relationship to the problem statement. Achieving the objective will, in fact, cope with the problem or need.

Is attainable with the amount of input you and the participants in the program can muster. Be realistic.

Can be attained within the time frame specified in the program.

Is clear and specific enough that it is possible to determine whether or not the objective has been attained. The result expected is something tangible or clearly identifiable.

Focuses on the most crucial parts of the program.

Makes a significant contribution to the carrying out of the fundamental responsibilities of your position.

Source: Boyle, Patrick A. *Planning Better Programs*. New York: McGraw-Hill, 1981, p. 201. Reprinted with permission.

ATTRIBUTES OF GOOD PROGRAM OBJECTIVES

Houle (1972) has outlined a number of attributes of objectives. Four of these seem applicable in developing training program objectives. The first is that program objectives are essentially rational and thus impose a logical pattern on the training function. This does not mean that the objectives describe all the possible outcomes of training over a specified period of time. No one set of objectives could be that comprehensive in scope. Nor will these objectives address the usually accepted, but often unstated, motives, aspirations, and goals of personnel who both plan and/or participate in training activities.

Second, good program objectives are practical and concrete. As practical guides for action, program objectives should neither describe things as they ideally should be, nor should they focus on esoteric problems that have no basis in reality. "The ultimate test of an objective is not validity but achievability" (Houle, 1972, p. 140).

Third, good objectives are discriminative. By stating one course of action, another is ruled out. For example, if training resources for the next calendar year are targeted at entry-level personnel, for the most part all other levels of personnel will be excluded from training activities. Whether this course of action is appropriate depends on a number of factors. For example, was training for this level of personnel seen as a priority need? Does management support this decision? Do the supervisors of the entry-level personnel believe the programs being planned meet the needs of their personnel?

The fourth attribute is program objectives may need to be changed during the training process. Practically speaking, this means training personnel must be willing to eliminate, revise, and/or add new program objectives as the situation warrants. This updating of program objectives should be done on at least a quarterly basis. This does not mean that training staff should modify or eliminate objectives just because they do not want to do them, or that they cannot be met as proposed. Judgment must be applied as to when it is or is not legitimate to revise the program objectives.

SUMMARY

1. Program objectives are statements of what is to be achieved by the training function. They provide concrete guidelines for program development and give both focus and direction to the program. They also serve as benchmarks against which the training function can be evaluated.

2. Program objectives describe expected or desired changes in the intended participants as a group or changes in the organization. Changes in the participants identify what they will learn and how their job performances should change. Changes in the organization relate to the maintenance and improvement of the training function itself and how training will benefit subsections of the organization or the organization as a whole.

3. It has often been said that good program objectives must be stated in measurable terms. Although it is helpful to have them written this way, it is not always possible or preferable. In addition, not all program outcomes can be anticipated, thus program objectives should be somewhat open ended so that unanticipated, but perhaps important, achievements of the program can be noted.

4. When developing program objectives, training personnel should start with the needs and ideas identified as priorities for training. Other personnel, such as the supervisors of trainees and the trainees themselves, should be asked to assist in the development process.

5. The wording of the program objectives should be applicable to the specific programming situation and should clearly communicate the proposed accomplishments of the program.

6. Four attitudes of good program objectives are given:
   a. Program objectives are essentially rational and thus impose a logical pattern on the training function.
   b. Program objectives are practical and concrete.
   c. Program objectives are discriminative in that by starting a course of action, another is ruled out.
   d. Program objectives may need to be changed during the training process.

►CHAPTER 8, WORKSHEET 1:
FOCUS OF PROGRAM OBJECTIVES

Based on your responsibilities as a training specialist, develop one broad program objective, as appropriate, directed at each of the following:

Participant's Learning: _____

_____

_____

_____

Change in Job Performances of Participants: _____

_____

_____

_____

Training Function: _____

_____

_____

_____

Organization as a Whole: _____

_____

_____

_____

▲ CHAPTER 8, WORKSHEET 2: CRITIQUING YOUR PROGRAM OBJECTIVES

List in the left-hand column at least five program objectives you have developed related to your training responsibilities. Does each of the objectives, in your opinion, meet the criteria for good objectives as proposed on the right half of the chart? Respond yes or no in the space provided.

Program Objectives	Is there a clear relationship between the objective and the problems/ideas/needs identified?	Does the objective make a significant contribution to carrying out the major responsibilities of your position?	Is the objective attainable in the time frame you have proposed?	Is the objective measurable?	Does the objective clearly communicate the proposed accomplishment?	Is the objective meaningful and can it be understood by all interested personnel?
1.						
2.						
3.						
4.						
5.						

9

DETERMINING POTENTIAL TRAINEES, THE PROGRAM FORMAT, AND STAFF

Carolyn C., a new training specialist, is now ready to design her first training program on personal computer spreadsheet applications for office practice. The content is one of the top three priorities for training that have been identified through a departmental needs assessment. Thus she feels confident that employees are interested and will attend sessions. But where does she start in planning the actual training event? Carolyn knows she must address basic items such as determining the format, scheduling, finding instructors, estimating costs, and locating facilities and equipment. But which task should she do first? Carolyn decides some assistance from Pam R., a colleague who is an experienced trainer, would be helpful. In talking over her dilemma with Pam, she discovers there is not any one order to the various tasks. Rather, each program planning situation and her own daily schedule will influence which task or tasks she might do first. Pam did stress to Carolyn that four major elements should be addressed at this point in the planning process:

1. Determining potential trainees, program format, and training staff
2. Handling all program arrangements and logistics
3. Preparing specific instructional plans
4. Formulating an evaluation component

No matter which task or tasks are initially undertaken the content for the program must be identified first. Depending on the complexity and comprehensiveness of the content, it may be divided into various subsections. For example, training staff may choose to offer only an introductory workshop on spreadsheet software or they may decide that a series of workshops over a six-month period focusing on the different applications of spreadsheets is really what is needed. Ideally, the content chosen should address the priority needs or ideas that have been identified earlier and should relate to the program objectives of the training function.

IDENTIFYING POTENTIAL TRAINEES

Having an idea of who the potential trainees are is usually the best starting place for putting together a specific training program. In addition, it is helpful to know what your financial resources, if any, are for planning, implementing, and evaluating the program. This latter topic will be discussed in detail in Chapter 10.

Completing a target population analysis, as described in Chapter 7, is one way to determine the characteristics of the potential trainees. This process assumes training personnel know which group or groups of employees in the organization will be interested in and eligible for training. If the criteria for eligibility have not been identified, this should be done first. Examples of such criteria might include job title and level, seniority, geographic location, and type of grouping wanted (e.g., homogeneous or heterogeneous). To review, the target population analysis involves answering the following questions:

1. How many people might be involved?
2. At what times might the potential participants be able to come to training?
3. Where are the potential participants located in the organization?
4. What are the ages of the potential participants?
5. What are the educational levels of the potential participants?
6. What can be assumed about the present and past job experiences of the potential participants?
7. What are the potential participants' motivations for training?
8. What are the costs (e.g., real dollars, loss of time on jobs) to the potential participants for attending the program? (Gane, 1972; Strother and Klus, 1982).

Obtaining the type of information asked for above is helpful to those planning programs for three primary reasons. First, knowing who the participants are and where they are located in the organization may make a difference in the delivery of the training. For example, delivering a program via teleconferencing may be more appropriate for a group of individuals in a widely dispersed geographic area than bringing them all together for a series of formal classes.

Second, selecting staff may be easier if training personnel have a good idea of who the potential participants are. Some groups prefer different presentation styles over others. Also, the background and experience of the instructor or facilitator may make one individual more credible than another to a specific work group. Third, knowing the potential audience will help in the marketing of the program because one of the first steps in marketing is determining the characteristics of the potential clientele.

DETERMINING THE FORMAT

Determining the format for the program is an important aspect of this phase of the program planning process. Format refers to the way in which training activities are structured and organized (Knowles, 1980; Lauffer, 1978). Three kinds of formats are used most often in training programs: (1) formats for individual learning; (2) formats for small group learning; and (3) formats for large group learning. Examples of specific learning formats that fit in each general category are given in Table 9.1. The material for the table was drawn from the work of Houle (1972), Knowles (1980), Lauffer (1978), and Robinson (1979).

It should be noted that these categories are not discrete in that some of the formats could easily fit into more than one category. For example, although a workshop is usually viewed as a small group activity, a workshop could also be for a large group of people. The large group would probably be divided into smaller work groups, so the flavor of the intensive interaction and product orientation would not be lost.

In choosing a format, six factors should be considered: (1) who are the participants, (2) availability of staff, (3) cost, (4) types of facilities and equipment, (5) program content, and (6) learning outcomes (e.g., knowledge, skill, attitude change). It is advisable to use a variety of formats in training as a wider range of styles and conditions for learning can be met when there is a choice of formats. "Besides, a variety of formats adds to the aesthetic quality of a program by giving it a sense of liveliness and rhythm, and a richer texture" (Knowles, 1980, p. 130).

TABLE 9.1. Training Formats Most Used

Category	Format	Descriptions
Individual	Apprenticeship	Formal or informal relationship between employer and employee by which the employee is trained for a craft or skill through practical experience under the supervision of experienced workers.
	Coaching	One-on-one learning by demonstration and practice, with immediate feedback, usually conducted by the employee's immediate supervisor.
	Programmed instruction	Use of programmed tests and booklets. Material is presented in a planned sequence of steps with immediate feedback given on the extent of person's learning.
	Computer-based instruction (CBI)	Computer-based instruction is a hardware and software system in which the computer software program teaches a student. Normally CBI is interactive with the student, who responds to questions from the computer and the computer modifies the instruction based on these responses.
	Independent reading/ study	Reading and study of selected materials (e.g., books, journals, trade materials) by individual learners. May receive assistance with this learning from other people (e.g., supervisor, teachers, librarian).
Small group	Course/class	A group with a definite enrollment that meets at predetermined times for the purpose of studying a specified subject matter under the direction of an instructor.
	Seminar	The focus is on learning from discussion of experiences and projects of group members. Participants in the group have sufficient knowledge and skill in the content material of the seminar. Instructor acts primarily as a resource person.
	Workshop	An intensive group activity that emphasizes the development of individual skills and competencies in a defined content area. Emphasis is placed on group participation and product output.
	Clinic	Session focuses on a single problem or skill in which participants present case illustrations of practice problems to an expert or panel of experts. The experts serve in consultant roles.
	Trip/tour	Taking a group of people to visit an object or place for on-site observation and learning.
Large group	Conference/ convention	One or more days of meetings with one of the primary purposes being education—to present information, exchange experiences, improve or learn new skills, and/or engage in problem-solving activities. Sessions include large and small group meetings with a variety of instructional strategies used.
	Institute	Intensive sessions, usually over several days, emphasizing the acquiring of knowledge and skill in a specialized area of practice.
	Lecture series	A series of presentations in which one or more speakers present materials on a given topic over a specified period of time.
	Exhibits	A stationary display of ideas, products, and/or processes.
	Telecommunications	Training sessions are sent via television or satellite disk to a variety of training sites. This may include voice-only teleconferencing, one-way video teleconferencing, or interactive video teleconferencing.

SCHEDULING THE PROGRAM

Once the format is chosen, training personnel can identify the appropriate length, the times for individual sessions, and potential dates for the program. Two examples of mock-up program schedules are given in Table 9.2.

TABLE 9.2. Sample Programs

Example 1: Schedule for Three-Day Conference

Day 1	Registration	10:00 A.M.-noon
	Opening luncheon with speaker	Noon-1:45 P.M.
	Session 1	2:00-3:15 P.M.
	Coffee break	3:15-3:45 P.M.
	Session 2	4:00-5:00 P.M.
	Reception	6:00-7:00 P.M.
	Dinner with entertainment	7:00-9:00 P.M.
Day 2	General session	8:30-10:00 A.M.
	Coffee break	10:00-10:30 A.M.
	Session 3	10:30-11:45 A.M.
	Luncheon	Noon-1:30 P.M.
	Session 4	2:00-4:30 P.M.
	Recreation	4:30-6:30 P.M.
	Banquet awards dinner	7:00-9:00 P.M.
	Reception	9:30-11:00 P.M.
Day 3	Session 5	9:00-10:15 A.M.
	Coffee break	10:15-10:45 A.M.
	Closing session and brunch	11:00 A.M.-1:00 P.M.

Example 2: Schedule for Tour

Time	Event
8:00 A.M.	Board mini-vans at main entrance
10:00 A.M.	Arrive at destination
10:00-11:00 A.M.	Coffee and overall introduction to organization
11:00 A.M.-12:30 P.M.	General tour of facilities
12:30-1:30 P.M.	Lunch in organization's cafeteria
1:30-3:30 P.M.	Choice of one of three in-depth visits to different operating divisions of the organization
3:30-4:00 P.M.	Wrap-up session
4:00 P.M.	Mini-vans leave for home organization
6:00 P.M.	Arrive at home organization

In finalizing the dates for the program, it is important that the times chosen fit into the participants' work, home, and family schedules (Houle, 1972). Few, if any, training activities should be scheduled around known peak work times. For example, to hold training sessions for managers or their secretaries during budget preparation time is not advisable. Programs should also not be planned on or near major holidays or vacation times, unless a family vacation option is offered as part of the training package.

IDENTIFYING PROGRAM STAFF

Staff are needed to design, coordinate, conduct, and evaluate training programs. One person may take on all these tasks or they may be divided among a number of people, depending on the size and complexity of the training function itself and the actual training program being planned. However the tasks are divided, training personnel must take on four major roles to get the job done: program designer, program coordinator, instructor/facilitator, and program evaluator (Houle, 1972; Lauffer, 1978; and Nadler, 1982). A description of each of these roles is provided in Table 9.3.

TABLE 9.3. Roles of Training Program Staff

Roles	Description
Program designer	Individual responsible for designing the program. This entails gathering needs and ideas for programs, setting program priorities, developing objectives, choosing formats, and developing instructional plans.
Program coordinator	Individual responsible for coordinating the program. Ensures all tasks related to planning, conducting, and evaluating the program are completed in a timely manner. Such tasks include making program schedules, arranging facilities, and registering participants. In carrying out this role, the individual may act as an information giver, broker, counselor, resources specialist, and/or administrator.
Instructor/ facilitator	Individual responsible for delivering the instruction on a one-to-one or group basis. Directly assists trainees to achieve their learning objectives using a variety of learning techniques and devices.
Program evaluator	Individual responsible for measuring and appraising the results of the program. Completes this task by specifying what will be judged, by whom, and on what criteria.

Some of the specific tasks (e.g., compiling lists of needs and ideas for programs, determining objectives and format) of the program designer have been discussed in Chapters 6, 7, and 8 and earlier in this chapter. A more detailed description of the other three roles (coordinator, instructor, evaluator) are given in Chapters 10, 11, and 12, respectively. The various tasks of the four roles are not necessarily discrete. For example, although the program coordinator usually arranges the facilities and equipment, the program designer may choose to do this task because of specific design requirements that the coordinator does not understand.

USE OF EXTERNAL STAFF

Program staff may be internal to the organization or they may be hired from the outside. Sometimes a mix of organizational personnel and external consultants are used. For example, while an internal staff person may coordinate and evaluate a training program, outside consultants may be responsible for the design and delivery of that program.

Munson (1984) has outlined five factors to consider in selecting external consultants:

1. *Caliber of the People*. Are the individuals both competent and capable? Will they be credible to your organization and the trainees?
2. *Quality of Their Materials*. Are the materials (e.g., audiovisual, workbooks) the outside consultants will use or develop be of good educational quality? Will these materials be useful to the participants?
3. *Adaptability*. Are the outside consultants willing to adapt their materials and/or their presentations to fit the specific needs of the buying organization?
4. *Scope and Depth of Available Resources*. Do the outside consultants add to the scope and depth of the present training resources of the organization?
5. *Cost*. Will the outside consultant cost more than using internal sources for the same activity? If so, is this additional cost justifiable?

There are two primary sources for locating outside staff: other organizations and private consulting firms. It is critical to check out the consultant carefully prior to signing a formal contract. This should involve face-to-face discussions, a review of materials, and, when possible, sitting in on a session the individual is conducting. In addition, information about prospective consultants can be gathered by talking with former clients and knowledgeable colleagues. For a university-based consultant, it is often helpful to also ask former students who are presently employed in the consultant's area of expertise.

TABLE 9.4. Negotiating Checklist

1. Clear and specific delineation of program or service to be provided
2. Program cost
3. Professional fees entailed
4. Expenses to be reimbursed
5. Other costs entailed (the facility, audiovisual equipment, shipping charges, etc.)
6. Commitment on named individual consultants to provide service
7. Participant evaluation
8. Participant completion certificates
9. Trainer certificates
10. Action steps to be taken
11. Schedule
12. Replacement of lost or damaged audiovisuals and leaders' guides
13. Cost of future educational materials
14. Training future trainers
15. Rights to use copyrighted materials
16. Termination

SOURCE: Munson, Lawrence S. *How To Conduct Training Seminars.* New York: McGraw-Hill, 1984, p. 59. Reprinted with permission.

Outside staff are usually paid in three different ways: pay per hour, pay per program, or percentage of income of a specific program (Knowles, 1980). No matter how they are paid, it is important to negotiate a written contract for services. Munson (1984) has supplied a very useful checklist to complete the negotiation process, as shown in Table 9.4. Negotiating a written contract will help promote a more harmonious relationship between the outside consultants and internal staff and, thus, will help ensure the desired results.

OBTAINING EFFECTIVE INSTRUCTORS/FACILITATORS

The instructor/facilitator has a key role in making a training event a success as he or she is responsible for assisting trainees to achieve their learning objectives. Therefore, it is very important to obtain effective personnel for this role. But how does one determine who will be good? Five selection criteria (Knowles 1980; and Munson, 1984) are outlined in Table 9.5.

TABLE 9.5. Criteria for Selecting Effective Instructors

Criteria	Illustration
Knowledge of subject matter	Instructors must be both knowledgeable about their subject matter and successful practitioners of their subject and/or skill.
Credibility	Instructors demonstrate their credibility based on their position, background, and/or personal impact. High credibility predisposes trainees to accept more readily the material presented.
Enthusiasm and commitment	Instructors should be enthusiastic about their subject and committed to teaching it to others.
Creativity	Instructors should be creative in thinking about techniques of teaching. They should be skilled in matching techniques to their subject matter and the audience.
Personal effectiveness	Instructors should be organized and prepared. They should be able to use humor effectively and have a genuine interest in whether or not the participants learn. They should also be able to adjust their presentations to the needs of the audience.

In choosing instructors, Giegold and Grindle (1983) have cautioned training specialists to be on the lookout for "Dr. Fox." Dr. Fox is an instructor "who has a wealth of personal charm, podium presence, and funny stories, but who conveys little else to the group" (Giegold and Grindle, 1983, p. 63). Audiences may react positively to this instructor, even though they learn little, if anything. Thus, although Dr. Fox may demonstrate creativity in teaching and personal effectiveness, he falls short of the other three criteria: knowledge of subject matter, credibility, and commitment to teaching.

SUMMARY

1. The content for the program must be identified. Depending on the complexity and comprehensiveness, it may be divided into various subsections. Ideally, the content chosen should address the priority needs or ideas and relate to the program objectives of the training function.
2. Having an idea of who the potential trainees are is usually the best starting place for putting together a specific training program. Completing a target population analysis is one way to determine the characteristics of the potential participants.

3. Determining the format for the program is an important aspect of the program planning process. Format refers to the way in which training activities are structured and organized. Three kinds of formats are used most often in training programs: individual, small group, and large group.

4. In choosing which format to use, six factors should be considered: participants, availability of staff, cost, types of facilities and equipment, program content, and learning outcomes. It is advisable to use a variety of formats in training.

5. Once the format is chosen, training personnel can identify the appropriate length, the times for individual sessions, and the potential dates for the program. In finalizing the dates for the program, it is important that the times chosen fit into the participants' work, home, and family schedules.

6. Training staff take on four major roles: program designer, program coordinator, instructor/facilitator, and program evaluator. One person may take on all these roles or they may be divided among a number of people. Program staff may be internal to the organization or they may be hired from the outside.

7. The instructor/facilitator has a key role in making a training event a success in that he or she is responsible for assisting trainees to achieve their learning objectives. Five selection criteria should be used when choosing instructors: knowledge of the subject matter, credibility, enthusiasm and commitment, creativity, and personal effectiveness.

▶ CHAPTER 9, WORKSHEET 1:
IDENTIFYING POTENTIAL TRAINEES

1. Identify a training program being developed by your organization. List the title and give a short description of that program.

   Title: _____

   _____

   Description: _____

   _____

   _____

2. Complete a target population analysis for that program by responding to the following questions:

Questions	Responses
1. How many people might be involved?	_____ _____
2. At what times might the potential participants be able to come to training?	_____ _____ _____ _____
3. Where are the potential participants located in the organization?	_____ _____ _____ _____

(continued)

Questions	Responses
4. What are the ages of the participants?	_____ _____
5. What are the educational levels of the potential participants?	_____ _____ _____
6. What can be assumed about the present and past job performances of the potential participants?	_____ _____ _____ _____ _____
7. What are the potential participants' motivation for training?	_____ _____ _____ _____ _____
8. What are the costs (e.g., real dollars, loss of time on job) to the potential participants for attending the program?	_____ _____ _____ _____ _____

1. Identify a training program being developed in your organization. List the title and give a short description of that program.

Title: _____

_____

Description: _____

_____

_____

_____

2. Using the following chart: (a) in column A, check all training formats that would be appropriate for the above program; and (b) in column B, put a star beside the format(s) you would use in this particular programming situation.

(continued)

Category	Format	(A) Appropriate Formats	(B) Format(s) You Would Use
Individual	**Apprenticeship** **Coaching** **Programmed instruction** **Computer-based instruction** **Independent study/reading**		
Small group	**Course/class** **Seminar** **Workshop** **Clinic** **Trip/tour**		
Large group	**Conference/ convention** **Institute** **Lecture series** **Exhibits** **Telecommunications**		

►CHAPTER 9, WORKSHEET 3: IDENTIFYING PROGRAM STAFF

1. Identify a training program being developed by your organization. List the title and give a short description of that program.

   Title: _____

   _____

   Description: _____

   _____

   _____

   _____

2. Using the following chart, identify specific staff (one or more persons) who will plan and carry out the program.

Staff Role	Identify Staff Internal or External to the Organization	Indentify Specific Person(s) to Carry Out Each Role
Program designer		
Program coordinator		
Instructor/ facilitator		
Program evaluator		

10

COORDINATING PROGRAM ARRANGEMENTS AND LOGISTICS

Training personnel are usually responsible for three major "behind the scenes" tasks in planning programs: preparing budgets, obtaining facilities and equipment, and marketing the program. These tasks may all be handled by one person or they may be divided up depending on the size of the staff available.

PREPARING PROGRAM BUDGETS

Preparing a program budget "is basically a process for translating intended activities into dollars and cents" (Strother and Klus, 1982, p. 207). Some training units are funded as a budget center and thus have organizational funds in addition to whatever income they may generate. Others operate on a cost basis and need to break even; while the remainder are required to be profit centers and make money (Nadler, 1982).

In working with budgets, some key words and phrases are used. One phrase is income and expense budget, the income side being whatever monies are generated to support training activities, and the expense side, the actual cost of developing and delivering those activities. Direct and indirect costs are also key words. Direct program costs are "out-of-pocket" expenses, such as external instructors' salaries, travel, and instructional materials. Indirect program costs are those expenses that do not cost actual dollars, such as space, administrative overhead, and equipment. What are usually considered indirect costs may become direct costs and vice versa, depending on the specific training situation.

For example: If a training program is held at the host organization's facilities, the space and equipment items are usually considered indirect costs, whereas if the program is housed at a motel or conference center, these same expenses are considered direct cost items.

Two other key terms are also used in relation to training budgets: profit and bottom line. Profit refers to making money, whether it is the training unit making money or the organization as a whole. As stated earlier, some organizations expect the training function to turn a profit. In addition, other organizations expect the results of training to have a positive effect on the overall profitability of that organization.

The bottom line refers to the amount of funds left after subtracting the expense from the income figures. This is calculated a number of different ways depending on the financial accounting system of the organization. Again, some organizations expect that training will have a positive effect on the bottom line of either specific units of the organization or the organization as a whole.

Determining the Cost of Training Programs

There are three basic costs associated with training programs: development costs, delivery costs, and evaluation costs (Laird, 1985; Warren, 1979). Expense items usually include staff salaries and benefits, instructional materials, facilities, equipment, travel, food, promotional materials, and general overhead (e.g., administrative, utilities). For some programs, all costs, except for the overhead costs, are direct costs; for others the costs are a mixture of direct and indirect costs. A sample worksheet for estimating program costs is outlined in Table 10.1. Not all items are cost items for every program. For example, some programs require the assistance of an outside consultant, others do not.

TABLE 10.1. Worksheet for Estimating Program Costs[a]

Budget Items	Development Costs	Delivery Costs	Evaluation Costs	Subtotal for Each Budget Item

Staff salaries
  Clerical
  Professional
  Outside consultants				

Staff benefits
  Clerical
  Professional				

TABLE 10.1. Worksheet for Estimating Program Costs [a] *(continued)*

Budget Items	Development Costs	Delivery Costs	Evaluation Costs	Subtotal for Each Budget Item
Instructional materials				
Films				
Videotapes				
Videodiscs				
Audiotapes				
35mm slides				
Overhead transparencies				
Manuals				
Handouts				
Computer programs				
Books and articles				
Other				
Facilities				
Meeting rooms				
Staff work rooms				
Hospitality areas				
Sleeping accommodations				
Staff				
Participants				
Food				
Meals				
Staff				
Participants				
Coffee breaks				
Other (e.g., cocktail hour)				
Travel				
Staff				
In-house				
External consultants				
Participants				
Equipment				
Promotional material				
General overhead				
Administrative costs				
Utilities				
Maintenance				
Other				
Other				
Subtotal for each type of cost				
			Total	

[a] Circle those items that represent indirect costs.

Laird (1985) has provided further guidance for estimating training development costs based on the U.S. Civil Service Commission's *A Training Cost Model* (1972) developed by the U.S. government. He first provides a formula for computing production costs for specific types of materials. A sampling of this material is:

Item	Formula	Total
Film	*Actual costs if purchased: $1,650 to $3,000 per minute to produce; $45 to $120 per ten minutes for prints*	_____
Audio Tapes	*$50 to $200 per minute to produce*	
	$2.50 per print to duplicate	
	$5 to $10 for commercial products	_____
35mm slides	*$15 to $50 per slide to produce*	
	$.45 per print to duplicate	_____

(LAIRD, 1985, P. 234)

In addition, Laird has outlined production costs by format (e.g., programmed instruction, computer-assisted instruction), the length of the course, and the methods used in relation to how much production time is usually needed.

Some organizations require that the trainee cost also be computed, either as a separate expense budget or as part of the total program budget. Although some of those items were included in Table 10.1, such as participant's travel and accommodations costs, others were not. Again, Laird (1985) has provided a useful formula for computing trainee costs:

Trainee costs:	*Total*
Number of trainees (by pay group) × median salary × training hours	_____
Number of trainees × hourly fringe benefit charges × hours	_____
Travel costs: Total from expense reports, or median cost × number of trainees	_____
Per diem: Total from expense reports, or median allowance × the number of trainees × number of days	_____
Student materials: Unit costs × number of trainees	_____
Trainee replacement costs: Number of hours × median salary	_____
Lost production: Value–per–unit × the number of lost units, or value–per–unit × the reduced production	_____

134

Faculty costs: _____

Number of trainers × *number of hours* ×
median salary   _____

Travel costs: Total tickets, or median ×
number of trainers   _____

*Per diem: Total from expense reports, or
median allowance* × *number of trainers* ×
number of days   _____

Special equipment or services:

*Rental of equipment: Total charges. If
purchased, amortize over 10 years.*   _____

$$TOTAL =$$ _____

(LAIRD, DUGAN *Approaches to Training and Development.*,©1985, ADDISON-WESLEY
PUBLISHING COMPANY, INC., READING, MASSACHUSETTS, P. 236.
REPRINTED WITH PERMISSION.)

In building the expense budget, it may be found that the costs are higher than the actual dollars the training personnel have to spend. Davis and McCallon (1974) have provided a list of strategies for limiting program costs:

1. Substitute less expensive instructional materials or eliminate certain materials altogether.
2. Reduce the number of staff needed to plan, conduct, and/or evaluate the program. Be especially cognizant of the cost of outside consultants.
3. Reduce the number of participants.
4. Employ a less expensive learning format and/or techniques so the same number or more participants could be involved.
5. Use a less expensive facility or one that will not cost you any direct dollars.
6. Have the program at a facility to which participants can commute so they do not have to pay for overnight accommodations.
7. Have participants pay for their own meals rather than having them be a part of the program package.
8. Require that participants find the cheapest mode of travel to and from the program (e.g., car pool, train vs. plane).
9. Change the program to a date when the prices for the facilities, meals, and so forth would be less (e.g., a weekend vs. a weekday, off-season for a resort area).
10. Make promotional material for the program less elaborate.
11. Shorten the program (e.g., from three to two days).

Determining How the Program Will Be Financed

The income sources for training programs vary depending on the type of institution (e.g., profit vs. nonprofit), the content and format of the program, and whether or not fees are charged for the program. The primary income sources for training programs are parent organization subsidy, participant fees, auxiliary enterprises and sales, grants and contracts, and government funds (Knowles, 1980; Strother and Klus, 1982), as pictured in Table 10.2.

TABLE 10.2. Primary Sources of Income for Training Programs

Source	Description	Example
Parent organization subsidy	The training function receives organizational operating funds.	The training department of Organization X receives an expense budget of $300,000 annually for salaries, materials and equipment, travel, general office supplies, and printing.
Participant fees	Participants are charged a fee for attending a program.	Eighty percent of all training activities must break even. Thus the participants' fees must cover all expenses for those programs.
Auxiliary enterprises and sales	Selling of materials and services provided by the training unit to other organizations and individuals.	Organization B has developed an excellent computer-based training program and is now selling it to other organizations for profit.
Grants and contracts from foundations and other private organizations	Private foundations and other private organizations award funds to a training unit to develop a specific training program. Usually these awards go to nonprofit organizations.	An award is given by a national foundation to a nonprofit hospital to develop a program on the prevention of heart disease.
Government funding (federal, state, and local)	Government funds are awarded or given to a training unit to develop a specific training program. These funds may be given to profit or nonprofit agencies depending on the regulations governing the funds.	Organization A is awarded a grant to initiate a job training program for unemployed workers.

TABLE 10.3. Worksheet for Estimating Income Sources

Source	Amount of Income/Subsidy
Parent organization subsidy	
Participant fees (fee × number of estimated participants)	
Auxiliary enterprises and sales (item or service to be sold × number of estimated customers)	
Grants and contracts (list each grant or contract with amount): 1. 2. 3.	
Government funds (list each source of funding with amount): 1. 2. 3.	
Total =	

It is important that training personnel have a good understanding of their funding sources and the policies and regulations that govern each source of funds.

Just as it is necessary to estimate the expense side of the budget, it is also necessary to account for the income side. This is especially so if one is expected to break even or make a profit on specified training events. A worksheet for estimating program income is displayed in Table 10.3.

Keeping Accurate Program Budget Records

It is important to keep accurate financial records. These records should be clear and yet be simple and practical. The type of available formal records depends on the accounting system of the organization in which the person is employed. Most organizations will have computerized systems, whereas some smaller organizations may still require manual entries. The specific system within an organization may not allow for program by program record keeping. Therefore, if records of income and expense for individual programs are desired, staff involved with training may need to develop their own set of books.

OBTAINING NEEDED FACILITIES AND EQUIPMENT

The environment in which training activities take place can affect the learning of participants. "A good environment can't assure success, but a poor one can mean failure" (Munson, 1984, p. 103). Consider the following two situations:

> SCENARIO ONE. Bob R. is attending a three-day workshop on organizational development at a resort lodge in the mountains. The weather has been beautiful, with the fall leaves at their peak color. He has really enjoyed his early morning walks from his lodging to the main conference center. He must admit though, he has been having a tough time concentrating on the materials, especially in those sessions held in Room 101, the one with the beautiful view. There are large windows on the sides of that room and it is hard not to look out every once in a while and do some planning for his upcoming fall hunting trip. Oh well! Maybe he will not have any sessions today in that room. You would think they would get curtains or something to hide the view, he thinks to himself.

> SCENARIO TWO. Sue P. is really enjoying this conference. The facilities are excellent, from the meeting rooms to the health club. Sue has thought to herself a number of times during the sessions that the meeting rooms must have been designed by conference goers like herself rather than some architect who spends most of the time in a comfortable office. The chairs are very comfortable, with just the right amount of padding; and the lighting is just right for note-taking. She can even see the board clearly as there is no glare. Sue also appreciates the fact that her hotel room is very quiet and comfortable, with a special security system for her floor. There is even a table she can work at and a hook-up for her computer. She must remember to send a note to the conference organizers and compliment them on their choice of facilities.

Obviously, Sue thought her learning environment was excellent and Bob was somewhat disappointed. A learning environment is defined by Finkel as:

> *every space in a facility in which meeting activities occur and the degree to which each detail of those spaces can be designed to contribute to higher levels of learning.*
> (FINKEL, 1984, P. 32)

The most important space for all training programs is the meeting room, whether it is designed for group or individual learning. In addition, training personnel must consider other space, such as places for meals and breaks, and, for longer programs, overnight accommodations and opportunities for recreation and socializing.

Types of Facilities Available

There are six types of facilities that are most often used for training activities:

1. Organizational training facilities
2. Organizational training rooms
3. Hotel and motel facilities
4. Conference and retreat centers
5. College and university facilities
6. Resort areas

Each type of facility has its advantages and disadvantages depending on the objectives of the training activity, the techniques to be used, who the participants and leaders are, the cost, how accessible the facility is, and the type of services provided by the facility (Finkel, 1984; Munson, 1984). For example, for a three-hour workshop for in- house personnel, using the training rooms of that organization would probably be the best choice of facilities. In conducting that same workshop for people from a wide geographic area, choosing a central meeting place in a local hotel facility or community college would probably work better.

In analyzing the type of facility needed for training programs of two or more days' duration, it is helpful to map out the estimated number of hours that will be spent in a 24-hour meeting day on various training activities. As seen in Table 10.4 Finkel has provided a useful chart for doing this:

TABLE 10.4. Form for Estimating the Number of Hours That Will Be Spent in a 24-Hour Period for Training and Personal Activities

Activities	Estimated Hours
1. Presentation and discussion in principal meeting room	_____
2. Work in small groups	_____
3. Coffee breaks	_____
4. Three meals	_____
5. Cocktail party	_____
6. Socializing with participants	_____
7. Recreation	_____
8. Individual work related to program	_____
9. Washing, dressing, writing personal letters, making personal calls, watching TV, reading	_____
10. Sleeping	_____
11. Making business calls or writing business letters	_____

SOURCE: Coleman Finkel, "Where Learning Happens." *Training and Development Journal*, *38*, (4), 34 (April 1984). Copyright 1984, *Training and Development Journal*, American Society for Training and Development. Reprinted with permission. All rights reserved.

Once this task has been done, it is easier to plan out what kinds of space (e.g., meeting rooms, break rooms) are needed and then translate those needs into choosing a specific facility.

If facilities need to be rented, it is important to check them thoroughly. As seen in Table 10.5 Munson has provided a useful facility checklist for doing this task:

TABLE 10.5. Seminar Facility Checklist

1. AVAILABILITY on seminar dates
2. COST
   a. Rooms
   b. Meals
   c. Seminar Room
3. TRANSPORTATION CONVENIENCE
   a. Public or own car
   b. If public:
      1. Convenience
      2. Frequency
      3. Cost
4. SEMINAR ROOM
   a. Size
   b. Appearance
   c. Lighting
   d. Decor
   e. Outlook
   f. Sound projecting
5. SUPPORTING SERVICES
   a. Food
   b. Sleeping accommodations
   c. Recreation
   d. Exercise facilities
   e. Public telephone
   f. Quality of service
6. OVERALL
   a. Scenic outlook
   b. General decor
   c. Cleanliness
   d. Experience in hosting seminars

SOURCE: Munson, Lawrence S. *How to Conduct Training Seminars.* New York: McGraw-Hill, 1984, pp. 115–116. Reprinted with permission.

Choosing Meeting Rooms

Different learning activities require meeting rooms to be arranged in different ways. For example, if an instructor wants to foster group interaction and team building, having chairs arranged in rows with people's backs to each other is not an effective way to do this. Rather, the placement of the chairs (e.g., around a table or in a circle) should ensure that participants have eye contact with each other. In addition, some types of learning activities require special facilities, such as space for prototype machinery or equipment.

The accent should be on detail in choosing meeting rooms. "Details that contribute to learning are kept or added; ones that hinder participant learning or leader effectiveness are changed or eliminated" (Finkel, 1986, p. 52). Important details or factors that should be checked when arranging for meeting room space are outlined in Table 10.6. This list and the recommendations for each factor are drawn from the works of Finkel (1986), Giegold and Grindle (1983), Laird (1985), and Munson (1984).

TABLE 10.6. Factors To Consider in Choosing Meeting Rooms

Factor	Recommendation
Room size	Avoid overcrowding or cavernous, oversized rooms.
Room structure	Ideal room structure is square. Watch out for long and narrow rooms and posts in the wrong places.
Windows	Choose a room with no windows or one in which the windows can be completely covered.
Furnishings	Make sure table and chairs are movable. Chairs should be padded and provide good back support.
Color	Look for pastel shades of green, blue, and yellow. Stay away from white and dark colors.
Adornments	Check to see if pictures, sculptures, or other types of adornment can be taken down.
Floor coverings	Floors should be carpeted in solid shades, not patterns.
Lighting	Look for indirect warm fluorescent lighting. Have rheostatic controls. For notetaking, a minimum of 30–40 ft. candles are recommended.
Glare	Eliminate all sources of glare.
Temperature	Keep temperature between 66 and 72 degrees. If you err, it is better to err on cool side. Be able to regulate the temperature.
Ventilation	Keep the air circulating in the room. Have no smoking.

TABLE 10.6. Factors To Consider in Choosing Meeting Rooms (continued)

Factor	Recommendation
Noise	Check for noise from heating and air-conditioning systems, adjoining rooms, corridors, and outside the building.
Acoustics	Check on the bounce and absorption of sound. Use different types of voices for this process.
Electrical outlets	Identify the location and type of outlets (e.g., three-prong outlets).
Computer hook-ups	Check for telephone jacks that would allow for computer hook-ups.

Reality does set in when selecting meeting rooms. There may be no real choice in which rooms are available. For example, a person may have to use the space available in their organization even though it does not present the best environment for learning. In situations like that, it is important to think how the available space can be used to its best advantage. If the lighting is poor, can extra lights be obtained for the session? If the placement of outlets is inconvenient, are extension cords available and how best can they be placed so people are not constantly tripping over them? If the room is too warm, could quiet fans be used to cool it down? Could more comfortable chairs be borrowed from another room just for this session?

How Can Meeting Rooms Be Arranged?

The question is often asked of training staff: "How do you want the meeting rooms arranged?" Often, the response is a quickly scribbled picture on a napkin or other scrap of paper. What would be more helpful would be to have a set of diagrams available to give to the persons responsible for arranging the room (e.g., custodial staff, convention center managers). Figures 10.1 and 10.2 provide sample diagrams of the most frequently used room arrangements:

FIGURE 10.1. Small meeting room arrangements. (Knowles, Malcolm, Reproduced from *The Modern Practice of Adult Education.* Copyright 1980, by Cambridge Book Company, 888 Seventh Avenue, New York, NY 10106. Reprinted with the permission of the publisher.)

SMALL MEETING ROOM ARANGEMENTS

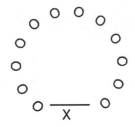

Chairs in a circle

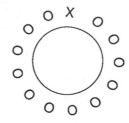

Chairs in a circle
around a table

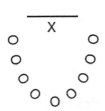

Chairs in a semicircle
or U shape

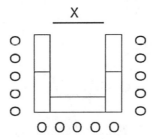

Chairs in a U shape
with table

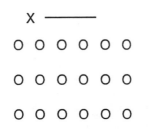

Theater style arrangement
with chairs

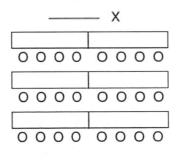

Theater style arrangement
with table and chairs

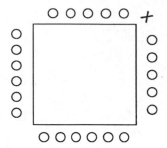

Chairs and tables in an
open, square arrangement

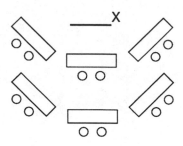

Chairs and tables in an
arch arrangement

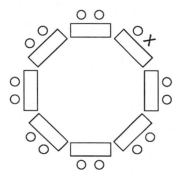

Tables and chairs in a
circular arrangement

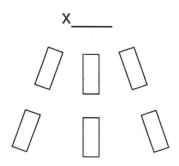

Tables and chairs
cabaret

144

FIGURE 10.2. Large meeting room arrangements. (Knowles, Malcolm, Reproduced from *The Modern Practice of Adult Education*. Copyright 1980, by Cambridge Book Company, 888 Seventh Avenue, New York, NY 10106. Reprinted with the permission of the publisher.)

LARGE MEETING ROOM ARRANGEMENTS

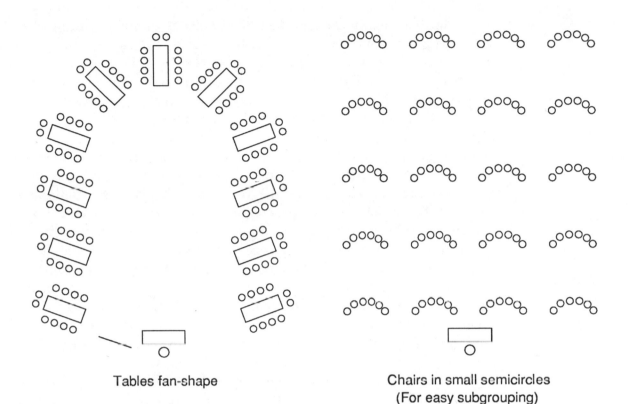

Tables fan-shape

Chairs in small semicircles
(For easy subgrouping)

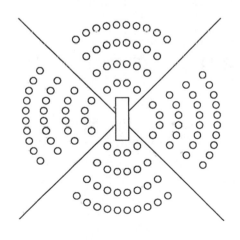

Theater-in-the-round
(or bowl)

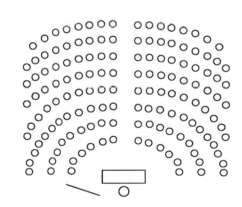

Semicircular theater

Arranging for Instructional Equipment

In arranging facilities, training personnel need to know whether the necessary instructional equipment (e.g., screens, overhead projectors, video players, easel pads, chalkboards) is available at the training site. For training programs held at the host organization, this usually involves scheduling the equipment. Equipment may also have to be borrowed or leased if the host organization does not own such equipment.

When renting facilities, the arranging of instructional equipment may be more complicated. Equipment may be supplied by the host organization, the presenter, the rental facility, or an outside rental agency as highlighted in Table 10.7.

Whether arranging for in-house or rental equipment three considerations must be taken into account: (1) Will the equipment be in good working order on the day of the program? (2) Will the equipment definitely be available at the times requested? (3) Who will be responsible for setting up and checking the equipment prior to presentation times? Past history can help in framing responses for items one and two. If the organization responsible for the equipment has a good track record for supplying working equipment in a timely manner, then training personnel can feel confident that this will be the case for their program. If, on the other hand, staff has heard that this organization's equipment has not worked properly and/or there has been scheduling difficulties, it is recommended that another company be brought in to manage the equipment for the program. Item three, that of setting up and checking the equipment, also needs to be decided up front when arranging for equipment. Will staff from the host organization be responsible for this task or will this be done by staff from the rental agency?

OBTAINING MANAGEMENT SUPPORT/APPROVAL FOR THE PROGRAM

The continued fostering of management support for training is an important job of training personnel. This includes all levels of management from a person's immediate supervisor to top management. Let's take the case of Peter Q.:

TABLE 10.7. Arranging for Instructional Equipment in Rental Facilities

Type of Arrangement	Advantages	Disadvantages
Supplied by host organization	The equipment usually will be in good working order. The program coordinator should have better control over scheduling and setting up the equipment.	Staff must be available to move and set up equipment in the rental facility. The program coordinator usually is responsible for making sure the equipment is set up properly and that it works.
Supplied by the presenter	The presenter feels most comfortable using his or her equipment. The presenter may be able to supply highly specialized equipment (e.g., CRT screens) that are not usually available.	Many presenters do not have easy access to the equipment. Some presenters do not want to bother carting their own equipment.
Supplied by the rental facility	The equipment is available on-site and therefore no arrangements need to be made to get the equipment to and from the host organization. Staff from the rental facility may handle all setting up and taking down of equipment.	The equipment may not be well maintained and thus may work poorly at best. Some control is lost by the program coordinator in setting up the equipment.
Supplied by outside rental agency	The equipment is transported to and from the training facility by the rental agency staff. Staff from the rental agency usually handle all setting up and taking down of equipment.	The equipment may not be well maintained and thus may work poorly at best. Some control is lost by the program coordinator in setting up the equipment. The program coordinator may not be familiar with how the rental equipment operates.

SCENARIO ONE. Peter Q., a new training specialist, has just completed most of the arrangements for an upcoming training workshop for entry-level managers and is ready to move full swing into the promotional phase. He is pleased with how the planning has gone thus far. Unfortunately he has not kept Pam, his supervisor, informed of his activities. He knows he should have, but he just has not had the time. Peter decides he should at least touch base with her prior to publicizing the event formally. Although Pam really likes his ideas, she does point out some possible major flaws, including the fact that the proposed speaker is not well thought of by the president of the company. Peter is glad to know of this concern at this stage because he is well aware that top management support is important to the success of the training operation.

In some organizations, personnel must receive approval from management before they can formally announce any training programs. The level of management approval varies from organization to organization, ranging from a person's immediate supervisor (e.g., department head) to someone two or three levels up in the organization (e.g., a vice president). It is critical to have a clear understanding, especially when dealing with controversial subject matter, of who has the authority to give the final approval for training programs.

MARKETING THE PROGRAM

It is very important in marketing a training program to have a clear picture of who the potential clientele are for the training activities (Hays, 1984; Shipp, 1981; Lauffer, 1978). For example, in planning a training program for entry-level managers, training personnel could assume that those entry-level managers are their prime clients or customers. This may be so, but other scenarios could also be built depending on the situation. The impetus for that particular training program may have come from the supervisors of these managers and thus a dual client system may exist of both the entry-level managers and their immediate supervisors. In this latter instance, the supervisors may be in fact the primary clients, with the entry-level managers secondary. Whoever the clientele are, it is necessary to seek out and respond to their needs and to have a clear understanding of how this clientele view the training activities and their possible benefits.

One way of developing a good picture of potential clientele, is to do a population analysis as described in Chapter 8. This analysis will yield a list of clientele characteristics, such as age, sex, educational background, type of employment, geographic location, and employment experience.

The Product, Price, Place, and Promotion

In addition to having a good picture of the clientele, four key aspects of marketing should be used by training personnel: product, price, place, and promotion (Farlow, 1979; Lauffer, 1978). Training personnel need to know their product, that is they need to be able to give a comprehensive and understandable description of the training programs for which they are responsible. They also need to be able to choose the right product (i.e., program) to fit the needs and desires of their clients.

If there is to be a cost charged to participants for a training program, then the right price must also be determined. How much is the potential customer, whether it be an individual or an organization, willing to pay? In thinking through costs, the cost to the participant for the training program itself must be considered, plus the participant's travel per diem expenses while attending. In addition, some organizations compute costs in terms of a participant's time away from the job.

In setting prices, the actual cost of developing and implementing the program, the demand for the program, and the competition should be taken into consideration (Lauffer, 1978). For example, lowering the price to increase the demand for a program may be a good decision, especially if the market is a highly competitive one. On the other hand, when the competition is marginal and the demand high, increasing the price may be appropriate.

Choosing the right place to offer a training program is also important. For example, hosting a three-day national conference in a place relatively inaccessible by air (which usually means higher airfares) usually is not a good decision, especially if the participants need to be able to obtain low airfares to attend the conference. Timing can also be key. Scheduling programs close to or on holidays can prove to be problematic to many trainees. The fourth key aspect of marketing, that of promotion, will be discussed in the next section.

Promoting Training Programs

Not all training activities need to be promoted. Some are mandatory— the supervisor says employees must go. Others are in such high demand that the job of the training personnel is to select participants from a large potential pool.

For the most part though, training personnel must promote or sell their programs to the potential audience. Many programs fail because of poor promotion. "People just never heard about them or did not realize how good they [the programs] were" (Knowles, 1980, p. 176) .

Promotion involves developing strategies and materials aimed at generating enrollments for training programs (Farlow, 1979). Examples of promotional materials used to foster interest in training programs (Farlow, 1979; Knowles, 1980) are given in Table 10.8.

TABLE 10.8. Types of Promotional Materials

Type	Description	How Distributed
Brochures	A written document describing a specific program or series of programs. A three-fold piece, measuring 4 x 9 inches, which can fit into a business-size envelope is used most often.	Direct mail Place in appropriate offices and public places (e.g., coffee room, cafeteria) Put in training packets to promote future training programs Hand out at appropriate meetings
Flyers	A single sheet, 8½ x 11 inches, promoting an activity or a group of related activities to people with specialized interests.	Direct mail Place on bulletin boards Put in training packets to promote future training programs
Form letters	Can be used in two ways: (1) as a cover letter mailed with a brochure or other promotional piece (the cover letter focuses the reader's attention to certain activities described in the promotional piece); and (2) as a separate mailing piece to make a personalized appeal to a specific group of people.	Direct mail
Posters	A sign used to attract attention about a specific training program or event. It should be attractive and eye-catching.	Place on bulletin boards and other appropriate places where prospective trainees might see it (e.g., office doors, in cafeteria, coffee room)
Newsletter/newspaper/ magazine ads	Placing an ad in appropriate publications announcing your program. There is usually a cost associated, except for local newsletters.	Distribution is by the organization who owns or is responsible for the publication
Newspaper/newsletter publicity	An information piece describing a specific program or series of activities.	Distribution is by the organization who owns or is responsible for the publication
Personnel	Having training staff, other organizational personnel, and/or past participants tell others about the program. This can be planned or done on an informal basis.	Individual in-person conversations, telephone conversations Announcements in group meetings

The Promotional Campaign

Having a clear picture of the clientele to be reached is an essential first step to any promotional campaign. For example, a promotional piece targeted at male managers may be poorly received, if in fact half of those managers are females. This does not have to be done in an overt way, but can come through in a more subtle manner, such as using only male figures in the brochure advertising the program.

Second, the actual promotional campaign needs to be planned. This involves building a promotional budget and then determining how that budget will be spent. Two examples illustrating this process are outlined in Table 10.9.

The third step is preparing and distributing the promotional material. The types of materials and how they are usually distributed was reviewed in Table 10.8. The most popular promotional materials used are brochures, flyers, and newsletters.

TABLE 10.9. Planning the Promotional Campaign

Name of Program	Target Clientele	Type of Promotional Material to Use	Target Time for Distribution	Proposed Cost
Example 1				
Time management (in-house program)	Entry-level managers	Flyers	November 1	$ 25.00
		Training newsletter	November newsletter	$150.00
		Word-of-mouth	Push two weeks prior to program	No cost
Example 2				
Computer-based management (ASTD workshop for area chapter)	For entry- and mid-level training managers	ASTD newsletter	January newsletter	$350.00
		Brochure mailed to all members	January 15	$200.00
		Word-of-mouth and telephone calls	Push three to four weeks before workshop	No cost

The writing of actual copy that is readable and attractive is key to this third step. Shipp (1981) has outlined four classic elements of a good promotional piece. The copy should: (1) secure attention; (2) create interest; (3) arouse desire; and (4) inspire action. He goes on to describe nine pointers for writing good promotional materials:

Keep it simple—use short sentences, familiar words, and contractions.

Use as few words as possible—say what you want to say, then quit.

Use the present tense, active voice—past tense and passive voice tend to drag.

Use personal pronouns—talk to the consumer just as you would to a friend.

Don't use cliches and don't over punctuate—this kills the copy flow.

Be careful about trying to use humor—it's difficult to manage and may create the wrong impression.

Don't brag—write from the consumer's point of view, not your own.

Concentrate—one benefit to one ad is optimal.

Write with enthusiasm—convince the consumer to share your excitement.
SOURCE: SHIPP, TRAVIS. "BUILDING A BETTER MOUSETRAP IN ADULT EDUCATION."
Lifelong Learning, The Adult Years. 5, (1), PP. 5-6, (SEPTEMBER 1981). REPRINTED WITH PERMISSION.

Farlow (1979) also suggests developing a fact sheet before developing the actual copy. The questions on the fact sheet are the same that need to be answered when preparing the actual program—Who? What? When? Where? Why? and How?

Your Promotional Assets

Farlow has provided a useful checklist (Table 10.10) for inventorying 15 tangible assets of the promotional process. She suggests these assets are needed to perform the process effectively. Each asset is rated as to whether the organization has it now, will have it, or must work at getting it.

TABLE 10.10. Tangible Assets of the Promotional Process

Have Now	Will Have	Must Work at	Tangible Program Assets
			1. The services of a professional publicity person
			2. A staff photographer and/or photo lab
			3. A staff artist and/or graphics person
			4. Personal and/or staff time which can be allocated without short-changing other responsibilities
			5. Other kinds of help—students, volunteer workers, steering committee or planning committee members, publicity pros and semipros at cosponsoring or cooperative institutions/agencies
			6. Access to a duplicating service or print shop Services available:
			a. Printing, duplicating of other sorts
			b. Folding
			c. Stapling
			d. Binding
			e. Collating
			f. Stuffing envelopes
			g. Preparing envelopes (pasting on preaddressed mailing labels, etc.)
			7. Access to a mailing center, which may offer the services above except duplicating, and which may also do ZIP-Coding and sorting
			8. A realistic amount of money for such "luxuries" as duplicating, postage, and help
			9. Access to a copying machine (fine for small numbers of reproductions) If the machine has special features (such as being able to duplicate addressed mailing labels so that you can have a number of sets at hand), this is a plus
			10. In-house access to the printed page or the airways (your newsletter, house organ, or bulletin, and those of your associates and cosponsor; a regular radio or TV spot, the broadcast of a related activity, in rare cases a sponsorship in local radio or TV)
			11. Special pages, sections, and programs related to education or your area of activity, to which you have ready access
			12. Access to an automatic typewriter[a]
			13. A good reference library of your own
			14. Access to more specialized reference materials
			15. Access to demographic studies or—much better—the counsel of a professional demographer

[a]In today's world a computer with a good word-processing system.

SOURCE: Farlow, Helen. *Publicizing and Promoting Programs.* New York: McGraw-Hill, 1979, pp. 26-27. Reprinted with permission.

SUMMARY

1. Training personnel are usually responsible for three major "behind the scenes" tasks in planning programs: (1) preparing program budgets, (2) obtaining facilities and equipment, and (3) marketing the program. These tasks may all be handled by one person or they may be divided up depending on the size of the staff available.

2. Preparing a program budget involves estimating the income and expenses for a program. Some training units are funded as budget centers, while others operate on a cost basis, and the remainder are required to be profit centers.

3. There are three basic costs associated with training programs: development costs, delivery costs, and evaluation costs. In addition, some organizations require that the trainer cost also be computed, either as a separate expense budget or as part of the total program budget.

4. The income sources for training programs vary depending on the type of institution, the content and format of the program, and whether fees are charged for the program. The primary sources of income for training programs are:
   a. Parent organization subsidy
   b. Participant fees
   c. Auxiliary enterprises and sales
   d. Grants and contracts
   e. Government funding

5. It is important to keep accurate, yet simple, financial records. The type of available formal records depends on the accounting system of the organization in which the person is employed.

6. The environment in which training activities take place can affect the learning of participants. The most important space for all training programs is the meeting room. In addition, training personnel must consider other needed space, such as facilities for meals and overnight accommodations.

7. There are six types of facilities that are most often used for training activities:
   a. Organizational training facilities
   b. Organizational training rooms
   c. Hotel and motel facilities
   d. Conference and retreat centers
   e. College and university facilities
   f. Resort areas

   If facilities need to be rented, it is important to check them thoroughly.

8. Different learning activities require meeting rooms to be arranged in different ways. In addition, some types of learning activities need special facilities, such as space for prototype machinery or equipment. The accent should be on details, such as room size, furnishings, lighting and noise factors, in choosing meeting rooms.

9. In arranging facilities, training personnel need to know whether the necessary instructional equipment is available at the training site. Instructional equipment may be supplied by the host organization, the presenter, the rental facility, or an outside rental agency.

10. The continued fostering of management support for training is an important job of training personnel. In some organizations, staff must receive approval from management before they can formally announce any training program.

11. It is very important in marketing a training program to have a clear picture of who the potential clientele are. In addition, four key aspects of marketing should be used by training personnel: product, price, place, and promotion.

12. Training personnel usually need to promote or sell their programs to the potential audience. Promotion involves developing strategies and materials aimed at generating enrollments. The most popular promotional materials used by training personnel are brochures, flyers, and newsletters.

Choose one training program within your organization and prepare an estimated expense budget for that program using the following chart. Leave a blank in the line if no costs are incurred for that item. First give the title and a short description of that program.

Title: _____

_____

Description: _____

_____

_____

_____

Budget Items	Develop-ment Costs	Delivery Costs	Evalua-tion Costs	Sub-total
Staff salaries				
Staff benefits				
Instruc-tional materials				
Facilities				
Food				
Travel				
Equip-ment				
Promo-tional material				
General overhead				
Other				
			Total	

1. Briefly describe a training program you will be coordinating in the next six months.

_____

_____

_____

_____

2. What type of facility would be the most preferable location for hosting the program? Describe your specific space needs for that choice.

Organizational Training Rooms: _____

_____

_____

Organizational Training Facility: _____

_____

_____

Hotel/Motel Facilities: _____

_____

_____

Conference/Retreat Center: _____

_____

_____

College/University Facilities: _____

_____

_____

Resort Area: _____

_____

_____

3. No meeting room is perfect. Knowing that, choose, from the list presented, your top seven requirements for you to label the room as adequate for a training event.

_____ The room is square

_____ The room has no windows

_____ The chairs are comfortable and movable and there is adequate table work space available for every participant

_____ The color of the room is a pale blue

_____ There are no distracting adornments in the room

_____ The floors are tastefully carpeted

_____ The lighting is good

_____ There are no sources of glare in the room

_____ The temperature of the room can be controlled

_____ There is good air circulation

_____ There is no background noise that might distract participants

_____ The acoustics of the room are good

_____ There are plenty of electrical outlets spaced adequately around the room

_____ There are convenient computer hook-ups

_____ The room is a good size for the number of participants

►CHAPTER 10, WORKSHEET 3:
PROMOTING THE PROGRAM

Choose at least two training programs for which you have responsibility for coordinating. Map out a promotional campaign for each of those programs, using the following chart.

Name of Program and Proposed Date	Target Clientele	Type(s) of Promotional Material To Use	Target Time for Distribution	Proposed Cost

11

PREPARING INSTRUCTIONAL PLANS

Preparing instructional units involves planning the interaction between the trainee and the instructor and/or the trainee and the resource materials for each training activity. Outlined in this plan are the learning objectives, content, instructional techniques, materials and equipment, and the evaluation procedures.

Instructional plans may be developed by the instructor of the training activity, the program coordinator, staff responsible for designing instructional units, or a combination of these people. The staff responsible may be internal to the organization or they may be hired as external consultants, as described in Chapter 9.

Often instructional plans are developed by one individual, usually the training instructor. This person may receive assistance in putting the plan together (e.g., gathering or designing resource materials), but the responsibility for the final product is on that instructor. In other situations, the design of the instructional plan is a team effort, especially when the training activities are very complex and comprehensive. For example, designing a training program for all line personnel in the use of new manufacturing equipment and machinery would probably be a team effort. The team members will vary, depending on the nature of the training activity, but usually at least three types of staff are involved: an instructional designer, a subject matter specialist, and a person representing the training function (Nadler, 1982; Tracey, 1984).

CATEGORIES OF LEARNING OUTCOMES

In preparing instructional plans, it is important for the developer to have a clear picture of the proposed learning outcomes of the instructional unit. To review, there are three major categories of learning outcomes: acquisition of new knowledge, skill building, and attitude change (Laird, 1985; Nadler, 1982; Tracey, 1984). The following are examples of instructional objectives illustrating each category of learning outcome.

Learning Outcome	Sample Instructional Objectives
Knowledge acquisition	The participant will be able to define the terms "conflict and "conflict management" and outline a seven-step process for handling conflict situations.
Skill building	Given a specific conflict situation, the participant will be able to accurately demonstrate, through a role play, at least two alternative ways for handling the situation.
Attitude change	Given an on-the-job conflict situation between two staff members, the participant will demonstrate through behavior and specific actions that he or she is not afraid of handling a conflict situation.

All aspects of the instructional design, from writing the instructional objectives to choosing the instructional and evaluation techniques, hinge on the focus of these learning outcomes.

AN INTRODUCTION TO INSTRUCTIONAL OBJECTIVES

Instructional objectives describe the intended result of a specific training activity (Mager, 1984). These objectives must be selected carefully, as they set the tone and direction for what trainees will be expected to know or do at the end of a training session. Instructional objectives should be set in the context of the program objectives for the overall training function.

Instructional objectives are useful for four major reasons. They provide:

1. Consistency in the design of instruction
2. Guidelines for choosing course content and instructional methods
3. The basis for evaluating what the participants have learned (Mager, 1984; Tracey, 1984; Tyler, 1949)
4. Guides for students to help them organize their own learning

Forms of Instructional Objectives

It is recommended for most training situations that instructional objectives be stated in performance terms. Objectives stated in performance terms provide a description of a job-related act that learners are able to exhibit to be considered competent. Mager (1984) has described three components of useful objectives:

1. Performance—what the learner is expected to be able to do
2. Conditions—important conditions under which the performance is to occur
3. Criterion—the quality or level of performance that will be considered acceptable

"Though it is not always necessary to include the second condition [conditions under which the performance is to occur] and not always practical to include the third [the level of acceptable performance], the more you say about them, the better your objective will communicate." (Mager, 1984, p. 21.)

Although performance objectives are usually the most appropriate form of instructional objectives for training activities, not all learning outcomes can be stated in this manner. There are certain kinds of learning that cannot be described in behavioral or performance terms. "Especially is this likely to be true whenever judgment, creativity, confidence, analytic ability, sensitivity, and the like are components of the learning" (Knowles, 1980, p. 234). Whatever form of instructional objectives is used, it is key that those objectives have meaning for both the trainees and the instructor, are understandable, and provide a clear direction for the training activity.

Writing Performance Objectives

As with program objectives, instructional objectives should be "stated clearly enough to indicate to all rational minds exactly what is intended" (Houle, 1972, p. 149). Tracey (1984) has outlined five general rules for communicating objectives clearly and correctly:

1. Avoid unfamiliar words
2. Do not confuse or misuse words
3. Be terse
4. Seek simplicity
5. Read what you write to make sure that it is what you mean to say

In writing instructional objectives, the focus of the objective should be the learner. Therefore, the objective should be stated in terms of what the learner will be able to know or do. The opening statement (e.g., "The participant will be able to . . .") should be followed by an action verb and then a content reference that describes the subject being taught. A sample list of action verbs by categories of learning outcomes is given in Table 11.1.

TABLE 11.1. Sample List of Action Verbs by Categories of Learning Outcomes

Knowledge Acquisition and Utilization	Skill Building	Attitude Change
To identify	To demonstrate	To challenge
To list	To produce	To defend
To compare and contrast	To calculate	To judge
To describe	To adjust	To question
To state	To install	To accept
To differentiate	To assemble	To adopt
To prepare	To operate	To advocate
To recall	To detect	To bargain
To classify	To locate	To cooperate
To categorize	To isolate	To endorse
To chart	To arrange	To justify
To rank	To build	To persuade
To distinguish	To conduct	To resolve
To explain	To detect	To select
To outline	To execute	To dispute
To analyze	To fix	
To evaluate	To lay out	
To formulate	To perform	
To investigate	To sort	
To modify		
To report		

Thus three parts—a statement of who the learning is for, the action verb, and the subject matter—are essential elements of all instructional objectives.

Some sample objectives with these three elements are:

The Learner	Action Verb	Content
The participant will be able	To detect	When the new equipment is not operating at 80 percent efficiency
The trainee will be able	To demonstrate	Effective and efficient use of parts one and two of the newly installed word-processing program
The learner will be able	To describe	The potential benefits of quality circles

As mentioned earlier, Mager (1984) recommends that two additional components, when practical and needed, also be included in instructional objectives. These are the conditions under which the behavior is to occur and the criteria for acceptable performance.

Examples of sample wording for these latter two components are:

Conditions Under which Behavior Is to Occur (What's Given)	Criteria for Acceptable Performance (How fast, how often, how well, how much)
Given a problem of the following type . . .	. . . 98 percent accuracy
Given a list of . . .	. . . 16 out of 20 correct
When provided with a specific set of tools . . .	. . . in a 20-minute time period
Without the use of any reference material . . .	. . . by brief responses (fewer than five sentences)
By checking a machinery chart next to the proper equipment . . .	. . . with no mistakes
When a customer is angry or upset . . .	. . . with all irate customers

Laird (1985, p. 11) gives a useful final word of advice on writing instructional objectives:

To the degree that the learning can be specified, instructors have a better bias for making good decisions while teaching . . . learners have a better sense of why and how well they are learning—the organization has a better idea of what it is getting back from its training investment.

SELECTING AND SEQUENCING CONTENT

Selecting the content involves choosing what will be learned during a training activity. The content is what a trainee must know, do, or feel to achieve the instructional objectives that have been outlined. Rarely can an instructor include all the material he or she would like to teach. Rather, instructors are limited by the time available, the format, the background of the participants, and the material readily available.

The starting point for selecting content is the instructional objectives. Tracey (1984) recommends preparing a rough draft of the content following each objective. He then suggests this draft be expanded until a detailed statement of content is produced. Especially when there are time constraints imposed, it is useful to prioritize the content in terms of its importance and relevance (Nadler, 1984). Smith and Delahaye (1983) have provided a helpful way to do this:

1. *What Must Know*. Essential to the objectives
2. *What Should Know*. Supplements the essential material and should be included if time
3. *What Could Know*. Interesting and relevant, but not essential for clear understanding

As Tracey (1984) cautions, care must be taken to avoid leaving out important points, overemphasizing topics that do not merit it, and repeating or overlapping the material presented.

Sequencing is the order in which the content should be delivered. There is no one set way to order content. For example, should the content be general to specific or vice versa or should it be abstract to the concrete or again the reverse? The ordering of the content depends on the participants and the nature of the content itself (Houle, 1972; Nadler, 1982).

A number of general guidelines for sequencing content have been outlined by Tracey:

Start the sequence with materials that are familiar to the trainees and then proceed to new materials.

Proceed from the simple to the complex, from the concrete to the abstract.

Teach trainees a context or framework to use in organizing what they are to learn.

Place easily learned tasks early in the sequence.

Introduce broad concepts and technical terms that have application throughout the training system early in the sequence.

Place practical application of concepts and principles close to the point of the initial development of the concepts and principles.

Place prerequisite knowledge and skills in the sequence prior to the point where they must be combined with subsequent knowledge and skills and applied.

Provide for practice and review of skills and knowledge that are essential parts of later tasks.

Introduce a concept or skill in the task in which it is most frequently used.

Structure objectives into closely related, self-contained groups.

Do not overload any task with elements that are difficult to learn.

Provide for practice of required skills and review of concepts and principles in areas where transfer of identical or related skills is not likely to occur unaided.

Place complex or cumulative skills late in the sequence.

SELECTING INSTRUCTIONAL TECHNIQUES

How does an instructor decide which instructional technique might best fit a specific situation? Let us take the case of Paul R., a training specialist for a large department store. Paul has set up a two-hour training session for all part-time salespersonnel who have been hired to handle the Christmas rush. He knows he will have both experienced salespersons and people who have never sold before. He anticipates about 25 people will attend the session. Paul has outlined what he believes to be a good set of instructional objectives on areas such as customer relations, selling techniques, and general store operations. He is now trying to decide just how he should cover such a broad content in a short period of time. He has outlined two possible alternatives. The first is to use a combination of lecture and small and large group discussions. He would ask the more experienced persons to serve as resource people and leaders in the small groups. His second idea is to use role playing, followed by small group and large group discussions. Then he would fill in with lecture material as needed. Paul decides to review his ideas with three of his experienced sales staff. He believes an offer of a paid lunch would entice them to help him out.

Underlying Paul's decision in choosing which instructional techniques to use is the assumption that there is no one best way of assisting people to learn (Houle, 1972; Robinson, 1979). Rather, there are seven major factors that should be taken into consideration when choosing instructional techniques (Houle, 1972; Laird, 1985; Nadler, 1982; Tracey, 1984; Warren, 1979). These factors are:

1. *Instructional Objectives*. Is the focus of the objective knowledge acquisition, skill building, or attitude change?

2. *Instructor*. Is the instructor capable of using the technique and does he or she feel comfortable in doing so?

3. *Content*. Is the content material abstract or concrete? What is the level of complexity and comprehensiveness of the material?

4. *Trainees*. How many trainees will there be? What expectations do the trainees have in terms of the techniques to be used and are they capable of learning through those techniques?

5. *Time*. What time period is available?

6. *Cost*. Are the costs, if any, associated with the techniques chosen realistic?

7. *Space, Equipment, and Material*. Is the space, equipment, and/or material necessary to use the techniques readily available?

Key Factors in Selecting Instructional Techniques

Of the seven factors to consider when choosing instructional techniques, the two key factors are the focus of the instructional objectives and the capability of the instructor to use the chosen technique. A list of instructional techniques appropriate for each category of learning outcomes—knowledge acquisition, skill building, and attitude change (Knowles, 1980; Laird, 1985; Nadler, 1982; Robinson, 1979; Tracey, 1984) are given in Table 11.2.

TABLE 11.2. Selected Instructional Techniques by Category of Learning Outcomes

Learning Outcome	Instructional Technique	Description
Knowledge acquisition	Lecture	A one-way, organized, formal talk given by a resource person for the purpose of presenting a series of events, facts, concepts, or principles.
	Panel	A group of three to eight people present their views on a particular topic or problem.
	Debate	A presentation of conflicting views by two people or two teams of people for the purpose of clarifying the argument between them.
	Group discussion	A group of 5 to 20 people have a relatively unstructured exchange of ideas about a specific problem or issue.
	Buzz groups	The dividing up of a large group into small "huddle" groups for the purpose of discussing the problem or subject matter at hand.
	Reaction panel	A panel of three or four participants react to a presentation by an individual or group of individuals.
	Screened speech	Small groups of participants develop questions they wish resource persons to respond to extemporaneously.
	Symposium	A series of related speeches (three to six) by persons qualified to speak on different phases of a single subject or problem.

TABLE 11.2. Selected Instructional Techniques by Category of Learning Outcomes *(continued)*

Learning Outcome	Instructional Technique	Description
	Listening groups	In groups, participants are asked to listen and observe an assigned part of a speech, panel, or the like.
	Demonstration	A resource person performs an operation or a job, showing others how to do a specified task.
Skill building	Case study	Written or oral presentation of an event, incident, or situation for a small group to analyze and solve.
	Demonstration with return demonstration	A resource person performs an operation or a job, showing others how to do a specified task. The participants then practice the same task.
	Games	An activity characterized by structured competition to provide opportunity to practice specific skills (e.g., decision making).
	Simulation	A learning environment that simulates the real setting in which the skills are required.
	In-basket exercises	A form of simulation that focuses on the "paper symptoms" of a job. Participants respond to material people might have in their in-baskets.
	Action mazes	A case study that has been programmed, involving a series of decision points with options at each point.
	Skill practice exercises	Repeated performance of a skill with or without the aid of an instructor.

Learning Outcome	Instructional Technique	Description
	Behavior modeling	A model or ideal enactment of a desired behavior presented via an instructor, a videotape, or film. This is usually followed by a practice session on the behavior.
Attitude change	Role playing	The spontaneous dramatization of a situation or problem followed by a group discussion.
	Simulation	A learning environment that simulates a real setting with the focus on attitudes and values related to the situation presented.
	Group discussion	A group of 5 to 12 people have a relatively unstructured exchange of ideas focused on the attitudes and values they hold relative to a specific issue or problem.
	Games	An activity characterized by structured competition to provide insight into the attitudes, values, and interests of the participants.
	Exercises, structured experiences	Planned exercises or experiences, usually using some instrument or guide, followed by a discussion of the participants' feelings and reactions.
	Critical incident	Participants are asked to describe an important incident related to their work lives. This is then used as a base for analysis.
	Sensitivity training (T-groups, laboratory groups)	A group of people assist each other with self-disclosure and feedback. The learning focuses on group process and interpersonal relations.

Although the categorization of techniques outlined is a good representation of how each instructional technique fits with a type of learning outcome, in actual use the categories of techniques are not that clear-cut. One technique may be appropriate for two or three of the categories of learning outcomes. For example, as shown in Table 11.2, group discussion could be used in both the knowledge and attitude categories, while a demonstration could be used to both acquire knowledge and build skills.

The second key factor in choosing techniques, as stated earlier, is the capability of the instructor. Does the instructor have the skill and knowledge to handle the technique? Does he or she feel comfortable using it? As Houle (1972) has stated, the twin enemies of employing a technique are self-consciousness and obviousness of use by the instructor.

The "principle of participation" has also been stressed by Knowles. "Given the choice between two techniques, choose the one involving the students in the most active participation" (Knowles, 1980, p. 240). A sample of techniques with high, medium, and low trainee involvement is given in Table 11.3.

TABLE 11.3. A Sample of Instructional Techniques with High, Medium, and Low Trainee Involvement

Trainee Involvement Level	Training Techniques
High participant involvement	Group discussion
	Buzz groups
	Case study
	Games
	Simulations
	In-basket exercises
	Structured experiences
	Critical incident
	Sensitivity training
Medium participant involvement	Reaction panel
	Screened speech
	Listening groups
	Action mazes
	Behavior modeling
	Role playing
Low participant involvement	Lecture
	Panel
	Symposium
	Demonstration

SELECTING INSTRUCTIONAL MATERIALS

Carol B., a new training specialist, attends a half-day workshop on the use of audiovisual (AV) materials in training. She really gets turned on to the use of these materials and decides to incorporate them into her training programs as often as she can. Carol's colleagues can always tell who is instructing a particular training session by the amount of AV equipment and handouts in the training room. To Carol's surprise, she finds that not all trainees are receptive to her use of the AV materials and she wonders why. Carol sincerely thinks they make her presentations much more interesting and lively, but she wonders if she is doing the right thing.

According to Tracey (1984), there are five selection guidelines for choosing training aids:

1. Select aids that fit the maturity, interest, and abilities of the participants
2. Select aids that fit with a particular learning activity
3. Maintain a balance in the type of aids used
4. Avoid the overuse of aids
5. Select aids that complement rather than duplicate other learning resources available

Based on Tracey's criteria, Carol B. violated at least two, if not more, of these basic guidelines—avoiding the overuse of aids and selecting aids that fit with a particular learning activity.

Types of Materials and Aids Available

There are a variety of instructional materials and aids that are used in training programs. A listing of the most popular materials (Robinson, 1979; Schall and Douglass, 1985; Tracey, 1984) are:

Instructional Aids

Worksheets, content outlines, observation guides
Workbooks, manuals, programmed texts
Books, articles, pamphlets, newspapers
Flipcharts, chalkboards, whiteboards
Models, objectives, mock-ups, specimens
Photographs, maps, charts, diagrams
Transparencies, slides, filmstrips
Audiotapes, records
Films, videotapes, videodiscs, television

Again, the type of materials and aids should be selected carefully to enhance the learning efforts of the participants.

Buying or Making Instructional Materials

Before developing or buying new materials, the training staff should explore what materials already exist in-house. Are there suitable materials available that could be adopted as is or with some modification (Schall and Douglass, 1985)? If not, is there competent staff available to develop the needed materials and if so, will it be more cost-effective to make the materials in-house or buy them from an external vendor?

If the decision is to make the materials in-house, this can be done in a number of ways. For fairly simple materials, such as worksheets and content outlines, the instructor or the coordinator of the program may develop the materials. The same is now true for transparencies, charts, and diagrams, especially if the trainer has access to a computer graphics or word-processing program.

When preparing more elaborate materials, such as programmed texts and videotapes, a more complex process is used, usually involving a team effort. A typical team is composed of a training specialist, a content expert, and an instructional designer (Tracey, 1984). The team's role is to plan and oversee the production of the needed materials. Individual members of the team, depending on their expertise, may do the actual production activities. It is important to validate the materials developed with actual trainees prior to using them on a large-scale basis (Schall and Douglass, 1985; Tracey, 1984). The validation process may be done with individuals or with a group, depending on the nature of the materials developed and how they will be used.

If the decision is made to buy all or part of the materials for a training program, Nadler (1982, p. 141) has suggested five useful questions for exploring possible restrictions on the use of those materials:

1. Can the program (or materials) be bought outright?
2. Are there any restrictions on the use of the materials?
3. Must subsequent use be authorized by the vendor?
4. What is the cost for subsequent use?
5. Can the learning materials be reproduced by the designer or must supplies continually be purchased from the vendor?

Nadler (1982) also cautions that it is unusual when materials purchased from outside vendors meet all the requirements of a particular program. Thus modifications may have to be made to the materials themselves or to the training program. For example, the sequencing of content of a particular program may need to be changed to match more closely the sequence of the purchased materials.

Whether the decision is made to use or prepare in-house materials or obtain materials from an outside source, "the major criterion of selection is simply this: Will it advance learning; is it needed? A training aid must actually aid learning and not be more 'eye wash' " (Tracey, 1984, p. 292).

DEVELOPING THE INSTRUCTIONAL EVALUATION COMPONENT

Instructional evaluation is a process for finding out if a training session actually produced the desired results. There are two major elements to this process:

The first is measurement, the determination by objective means of the extent to which learners have achieved the criteria of evaluation. The second part is appraisal, a subjective judgment of how well educational objectives have been achieved.

(HOULE, 1972, p. 182)

Mehrens and Lehmann (1978) have cited four important ways instructional evaluation procedures can aid the instructor:

1. Provides baseline data on entry-level knowledge, skills, and attitudes of learners
2. Aids in refining and clarifying the instructional objectives for the participants
3. Assists in evaluating the degree to which the instructional objectives have been achieved
4. Helps in the revision of the training activity itself (e.g., content, techniques)

Doing Instructional Evaluation

The starting point for instructional evaluation is the instructional objectives. The evaluation techniques chosen need to match the focus of those objectives–knowledge acquisition, skill building, or attitude change. A sample of the most widely used techniques for evaluating what has been learned in a training session is given in Table 11.4.

Although categorization is a helpful guide in choosing evaluation techniques, depending on how a technique is used, it may fit into more than one category of learning outcomes. For example, written tests, depending on the type of test items, could measure both knowledge acquisition and/or attitude change.

An acceptable evaluation technique has two primary characteristics: reliability and validity. A technique is valid if it measures what it is supposed to measure. For example, if you want trainees to show they can apply the knowledge learned to their job situations, then a test that measures the ability to recall facts is not an appropriate measure. Two ways of increasing validity are to: (1) have a team of content experts review the evaluation technique for content and construct validity; and (2) make sure the evaluation items relate directly to the instructional objectives.

TABLE 11.4. Selected Instructional Evaluation Techniques by Category of Learning Outcomes

Learning Outcome	Evaluation Technique	Description
Knowledge acquisition	Pencil and paper tests	Trainees respond to a printed set of questions. The test may consist of multiple choice, true–false, matching and/or sentence completion items.
	Essays	Trainees respond to one or more questions or problem situations to be answered in written form. They may be asked to compare, discuss, analyze, criticize, evaluate, or the like.
	Oral tests	Trainees are asked to respond to a set of questions orally, usually on an individual basis.
	Oral presentations	A trainee gives a formal oral presentation to a selected group on a specific topic area.
Skill building	Performance tests	Trainees are asked to perform a skill, operation, or practical application. Often specified equipment and/or materials are used. A clear statement of the standards required must be developed and all parties must understand those standards.
	On-the-job observations	Observations are made on-the-job of a set of performance behaviors. Again, clear standards for the performance must be set.
	Product reviews	A product produced by the trainee is reviewed by the instructor and/or an outside expert or panel of experts.

TABLE 11.4. Selected Instructional Evaluation Techniques by Category of Learning Outcomes *(continued)*

Attitude change	Role playing	Trainees are asked to role play a situation in which the focus of that role play is on the attitudes portrayed by the players.
	Pencil and paper tests	A printed set of questions to be answered by the participants. Items focus on specific attitudes. Although these items are difficult to construct, they can provide a very useful measure.
	Exercises	Trainees are asked to participate in exercises that display their attitudes about a particular topic or situation.

A reliable technique produces results that are consistent over time. One way to test for reliability is to administer the evaluation technique to a group of trainees twice, with no training in between. If the results are similar, then the technique can be considered at least partially reliable. However, no evaluation technique is perfectly reliable. Usually careful standards for administering and scoring, plus clear and concise test items will increase reliability (Smith and Delahaye, 1983; Tracey, 1984).

There are two primary ways to carry out instructional evaluation. The first is pretesting and posttesting, and the second is posttesting only. The pretest and posttest format allows the instructor to gather baseline data, which can help both in finalizing what material he or she will actually cover in the session, as well as measuring what has been learned.

Smith and Delahaye (1983, p. 108) have outlined four important points to consider when administering an instructional evaluation. First, many participants are very anxious about any type of testing situation. Training personnel need to respond to this anxiety with both concern and respect for the trainees' feelings. Second, clear and complete instructions about the evaluation should be provided. Specified should be:

The date, time, and place of the test; what the trainees can and/or should bring to the test with them, how long the test will last; the format of the test; and what the test will require the trainees to do.

Third, a comfortable test environment (e.g., heat, lighting) should be provided, and fourth, all materials (e.g., paper, pencils, equipment) the trainees will need to complete the evaluation should be available.

Instructor and Training Session Evaluation

In addition to the evaluation of the changes in participant's knowledge, skills, or attitudes, training personnel may also want to gather participant reactions to the training session itself. Was the session useful to them? Were the instructional techniques used appropriate? Was the instructor effective? What was especially good about the session versus what could be improved? A sample instructional reaction sheet is given in Table 11.5.

TABLE 11.5. A Sample Participant Reaction Sheet

Corporate Claims Development
Training Evaluation

Course _____ Instructor _____ Date _____

Please assist us in evaluating the quality of the instruction and the classroom facilities used for your course by completing this questionnaire. Please circle the number that best represents your views; 1 being negative, 4 being positive. Your specific comments and suggestions for improvement would be most appreciated.

Have you had prior experience and/or training in CAPS before? If so, what?

_____

_____

Part 1—Course Content	Low			High
Were the course objectives clearly evident to you? Comments/Suggestions: _____	1	2	3	4
Did you learn what you expected to learn? Comments/Suggestions: _____	1	2	3	4
Was the material presented relevant and valuable to you? Comments/Suggestions: _____	1	2	3	4
Was the material presented at an appropriate rate? Comments/Suggestions: _____	1	2	3	4
Was there an adequate amount of time allotted to topics? Comments/Suggestions: _____	1	2	3	4
Was the balance between lectures, discussions, and practical applications effective? Comments/Suggestions: _____	1	2	3	4

TABLE 11.5. A Sample Participant Reaction Sheet *(continued)*

Were the visual aids (transparencies, flipcharts, etc.) helpful to you?   1   2   3   4
    Comments/Suggestions: _____

_____

Was the course well organized, allowing a progression from one topic to another?   1   2   3   4
    Comments/Suggestions: _____

_____

Do you feel you mastered the subject matter of this course?   1   2   3   4
    Comments/Suggestions: _____

_____

How do you rate this course overall?   1   2   3   4
    Comments/Suggestions: _____

_____

Part 2—Trainer Skills

Was the trainer enthusiastic?	1	2	3	4
Was the trainer always well prepared?	1	2	3	4
Did the trainer have an expert knowledge of the course content?	1	2	3	4
Did the trainer make an effort to help you feel comfortable?	1	2	3	4
Did the trainer provide you with adequate assistance?	1	2	3	4
Did the trainer have effective presentation skills?	1	2	3	4
Did the trainer define terms and concepts clearly?	1	2	3	4
Did the trainer give clear instructions for each exercise?	1	2	3	4
Did the trainer communicate well with the students?	1	2	3	4
Was the trainer able to stimulate group discussion?	1	2	3	4
Did the trainer stick to the time schedule?	1	2	3	4
How do you rate the trainer's skills overall?	1	2	3	4

Strong Features: _____

_____

Weak Features: _____

_____

Additional Suggestions for Improvement _____

_____

Thank You for Your Help!

Source: Rhonda Sadler, and Bruce Lindeman. *Training Policies, Corporate Claims Development.* Richmond, VA: Blue Cross and Blue Shield of Virginia, 1987. Reprinted with permission.

PREPARING LESSON PLANS

The lesson plan combines into one document all of the elements that go into preparing an instructional plan: the instructional objectives, the content, the instructional techniques and materials, and the evaluation component. When clearly and concisely developed, lesson plans provide road maps for instructors to get them where they want to go and remind them how they have decided to get there. Two major advantages of preparing lesson plans are that they help instructors "time" the various parts of the training activity and they show instructors where to pick up and continue the activity if they get too far "off course" (Smith and Delahaye, 1983).

There is no set form for a lesson plan as long as the major components of the activity are outlined:

1. Instructional objectives
2. Content—key points to emphasize
3. Techniques and materials to be used
4. Evaluation plan
5. Estimated time for each major part of the learning activity

A sample lesson plan is given in Table 11.6.

TABLE 11.6. Sample Lesson Plan

Session Title: A Program Development Model: A Checklist for Planning Successful Programs
Date and Time: Wednesday, 10:00 A.M.–Noon

Instructional Objectives	Content Heading	Key Points To Be Emphasized	Instructional Techniques	Estimated Time
The participants will be able to:				
Describe an 11-component program development model	Program development model	Model is set of interacting and dynamic elements. Most program planners work concurrently on a number of the components. Describe the 11 components of the model. Key word in using the model is flexibility.	Lecture Question-and-answer period	30 minutes

TABLE 11.6. Sample Lesson Plan (continued)

Session Title: A Program Development Model: A Checklist for Planning Successful Programs
Date and Time: Wednesday, 10:00 A.M.–Noon

Instructional Objectives	Content Heading	Key Points To Be Emphasized	Instructional Techniques	Estimated Time
Analyze a case study using the model presented	Analyze case study	In small group of five people analyze case study. Appoint a discussion leader and a recorder. Report back to the whole the results of each small group's work.	Small group discussion Report from small groups Large group discussion	45 minutes
Critique the model in terms of its usefulness for on-the-job applications	Critique the model	Strengths and weaknesses of the model. How could the model be revised?	Buzz groups Large group discussion	30 minutes

Evaluation: <u>Pretest and posttest on the program development model</u>
                <u>Review of the case study analysis</u>

Instructional Materials and Equipment Needed

For Instructor	For Trainees
Overhead projector	Handouts
Overheads	1. Article on program development model
	2. Case study
	3. Critique form
	4. Reference list on program development

Room Arrangement Needed: <u>Chairs arranged around tables, table</u>
                        <u>up front for the instructor</u>

General Notes/Comments: _____

SUMMARY

1. Preparing instructional units involves planning the interaction between the trainee and the instructor and/or the trainee and the resource materials. Outlined in the instructional plan are the learning objectives, content, instructional techniques, materials and equipment, and the evaluation procedures.

2. In preparing instructional plans, it is important for the developer to have a clear picture of the proposed learning outcomes. To review, there are three major categories of learning outcomes: acquisition of new knowledge; skill building; and attitude change. All aspects of the instructional design, from the writing of the instructional objectives to choosing the instructional and evaluation techniques, hinge on the focus of these learning outcomes.

3. Instructional objectives describe the intended result of the training activity. These objectives must be selected carefully as they set the tone and direction for what trainees will be expected to know or do at the end of the training session.

4. Although performance objectives are usually the most appropriate form of instructional objectives for training activities, not all learning outcomes can be stated in this manner, especially when creativity, analytic ability, sensitivity, and the like, are components of the learning.

5. In writing instructional objectives, the focus of an objective should be the learner. Therefore, the objective should be stated in terms of what the learner will be able to know or do. This should be followed by an action verb and then a content reference that describes the subject being taught.

6. Two additional components may also be included when practical and needed: (1) the conditions under which the behavior is to occur; and (2) the criteria for acceptable performance.

7. Selecting the content involves choosing what will be learned during a training activity. The starting point for selecting content is the instructional objectives. Sequencing is the order in which the content is delivered.

8. There are seven major factors that should be taken into consideration when choosing instructional techniques:
   a. The instructional objectives
   b. The instructor's capability
   c. The content
   d. The trainee
   e. The time available
   f. The cost
   g. The available space, equipment, and material
   The two key factors are the focus of the instructional objectives and the instructor's capability.

9. Examples of instructional techniques appropriate for each category of learning outcome are:
   a. Knowledge Acquisition—lecture, panel debate, buzz groups
   b. Skill Building—case study, games, skill practice exercises
   c. Attitude Change—role play, group discussion, sensitivity training

10. There are a variety of instructional materials and aids that are used in training programs from worksheets to videodiscs. These materials and aids may be prepared in-house or obtained from an outside source.

11. Instructional evaluation is a process for finding out if a training session actually produced the desired results. It involves both measurement and appraisal.

12. The evaluation techniques chosen need to match the focus of the instructional objectives. Examples of instructional techniques appropriate for each category of learning outcome are:
   a. Knowledge Acquisition—paper and pencil tests, essays, oral presentations
   b. Skill Building—performance tests, on-the-job observations
   c. Attitude Change—role playing, exercises, tests

13. An acceptable evaluation technique has two primary characteristics: reliability and validity. A technique is valid if it measures what it is supposed to measure. A reliable technique produces results that are consistent over time.

14. The lesson plan combines into one document all the elements that go into preparing an instructional plan: the instructional objectives, the content, the instructional techniques and materials, and the evaluation component. When clearly and concisely developed, the lesson plan provides a road map for the instructor.

Describe briefly a training session for which you will act as the instructor.

_____

_____

_____

_____

Develop a set of instructional objectives for that session using the following format. Complete each part for each objective, as appropriate.

The Learner	Action Verb	Content	Conditions Under which the Behavior Is To Occur	Criteria for Acceptable Performance

►CHAPTER 11, WORKSHEET 2: SELECTING INSTRUCTIONAL TECHNIQUES

For the same training session you described in Worksheet 1, develop two alternative ways the material could be taught. In doing this task keep in mind the focus of the learning outcomes and what type of participant involvement you want.

Alternative 1: Outline of Instructional Technique(s) to Use

_____

_____

_____

_____

Alternative 2: Outline of Instructional Technique(s) to Use

_____

_____

_____

_____

▶ CHAPTER 11, WORKSHEET 3: COMPLETING A LESSON PLAN

Complete a lesson plan for a training session for which you will be serving as the instructor.

Lesson Plan Sheet

Session Title _____

Date and Time _____

Instructional Objectives	Content Heading	Key Points To Be Emphasized	Instructional Techniques	Estimated Time

Evaluation Plan: _____

_____

_____

_____

Instructional Materials and Equipment Needed

> *For Instructor*   *For Participants*

_____   _____

_____   _____

_____   _____

_____   _____

Room Arrangement Needed: _____

_____

_____

General Notes/Comments: _____

_____

_____

_____

12

FORMULATING A CONTINUOUS EVALUATION COMPONENT

John R. wants to demonstrate that he is doing a good job as the new training coordinator for the safety training program. His predecessor had this responsibility for years and ran a rather informal shop. Other than the big chart displaying the number of accident-free days for the company, no systematic records on the safety training program had ever been kept. There were some figures on the number and types of programs offered with the number of participants in each program, but the data was incomplete because the figures had not been kept for all programs. Also, there was a great deal of inconsistency in how the figures had been gathered and recorded. John had asked his predecessor if there were any evaluation reports on the program, and his predecessor's response was: "You'll know if they're bad cause the trainees and/or supervisors will tell you." John wonders how he can demonstrate that the safety program is doing what it is supposed to be doing—lowering the rate and severity of accidents in the plant.

John is not alone in inheriting a training program in which the evaluation of that program has been haphazard at best. Evaluation is an essential part of program development and yet it seldom receives the attention it deserves (Federal Highway Administration, 1977; Laird, 1985; Michalak and Yager, 1979).

PROGRAM EVALUATION DEFINED

Program evaluation is the process used to determine the effectiveness of the training activities and the results of those activities. Evaluation should be a continuous process, which begins in the design phase (Boyle, 1981; Laird, 1985; Nadler, 1982) and concludes with follow-up studies. The heart of program evaluation is judging the value or worth of a training program (Boyle, 1981; Federal Highway Administration, 1977; Houle, 1972). As with instructional evaluation, program evaluation involves the dual process of measurement and appraisal. Measurement is determining by some objective means whether the goals and objectives for the program have been achieved. Appraisal is the more subjective judgment of how well those program objectives have been accomplished and whether each objective was a worthwhile endeavor (Houle, 1972).

Doing program evaluation serves a number of purposes. More specifically, the process: (1) helps keep staff focused on the goals and objectives of the program, (2) provides information for decision making on all aspects of the program, (3) identifies the strengths and weaknesses of the program, (4) allows for program accountability, (5) provides data on the major accomplishments of the program, and (6) identifies ways of improving future programs (Boyle, 1981; Brandenburg, 1982; Kirkpatrick, 1976; Michalak and Yager, 1979; Strother and Klus, 1982). In essence, good program evaluation provides useful feedback to training personnel, participants, supervisors of participants, management, and other interested parties throughout the life of the program (Brandenburg, 1982; Nadler, 1982).

Although program evaluation is a desirable and necessary part of the programming process, Knowles (1980) has cautioned trainers of three major pitfalls. First, the outcomes of training programs may be too complicated and the number of variables affecting those outcomes too numerous to be able to prove that training alone actually produced the desired changes. For example, it appeared that a three-week training program increased the proficiency of office workers in the use of a new word-processing system. This conclusion was reached by comparing pretest and posttest scores of all workshop participants on the use of the system once the program was completed (the trainees meet for two hours per day twice a week). Yet, when the office workers were asked what the key element was that helped them to increase their proficiency, 95 percent of them responded that on-the-job trial and error was how they had mastered the system. The training program in fact had hindered their progress more than helped because the instructor often gave poor and incomplete descriptions of how to use the new package.

A second pitfall is that current evaluation procedures, however scientifically rigorous, may not be able to provide hard evidence that the more subtle, and at times the most important aspects of the training program, have been achieved. This is especially so for training programs on "soft skills," such as enhancing interpersonal relations or motivating employees. Third, conducting program evaluations cost time and money, neither of which some organizations are willing to provide "simply to document the worth of training which they can see is valuable" (Knowles, 1980, p. 199).

FOCUS OF PROGRAM EVALUATION

The program objectives serve as the basis for program evaluation. The purpose, design, and criteria should be drawn from these objectives. This does not mean that other aspects of the program not addressed by the program objectives should be excluded from the evaluation; rather, the program objectives should serve as the primary guidepost for the evaluation process.

Program objectives, as described in Chapter 8, focus on changes in: (1) the participants' learning; (2) the participants' job performances; (3) the organizational policies, practices, and functions; and (4) the training unit's policies, practices, and functions. Results of the program evaluation can demonstrate whether these changes actually occurred and if not, why? The changes to be examined closely mirror Kirkpatrick's (1976) four levels of evaluation: (1) reaction, (2) learning, (3) behavior, and (4) results. Examples of major evaluation questions and appropriate data gathering techniques, based on the focus of the evaluation, are given in Table 12.1 (Chalofsky, 1985; Kirkpatrick, 1976; Salinger and Deming, 1982). A more complete explanation of evaluation techniques is given later in this chapter.

Participant evaluation is the most generally used form of evaluation (Brandenburg, 1982; Kirkpatrick, 1976; Munson, 1984). Participants usually complete a short questionnaire at the end of training, indicating whether or not they liked the program. Trainees are asked their opinions on such items as content, instructor, instructional techniques, facilities, and food service. Another common evaluation indicator is reporting on: (1) the number of participants, (2) the number of hours in the program, and (3) the number of sessions and topics covered (Michalak and Yager, 1979). What is interesting about the two most commonly used sources of data for program evaluation is that they fall in the category of evaluating the training program itself. The major purpose of training—change in participants' job performances as a result of gaining new knowledge, skills, and/or attitudes—is not measured as often.

TABLE 12.1. Examples of Major Evaluation Questions and Appropriate Techniques To Use, Based on the Focus of the Evaluation

Focus of Evaluation	Major Question(s) Asked	Techniques Appropriate for Data Collection
Participants' learning	What knowledge, skills, and attitudes were learned by the participants?	Pencil and paper tests Performance tests Product evaluation Attitude surveys
Participants' job performances	What changes were made in participants' job performances as a result of the program? To what degree are those changes maintained over time?	Observations Written questionnaires Interviews Performance appraisals
Organizational policies, procedures, practices, and functions	What were the tangible results in relationship to the whole or subsections of the organization? (e.g., reduced costs, improved quantity, reduced turnover, less absenteeism)	Review appropriate records before and after training (e.g., productivity, absenteeism) Interviews Written questionnaires Cost-benefit analyses
Training unit's policies, procedures, practices, and functions	What improvements, if any, could be made in the program planning process? How well did the participants like the program? Are training personnel doing their jobs effectively? Does the value of the participants' improved performances meet or exceed the cost of training? Is the training program administered in an effective and efficient manner?	Written questionnaires Interviews (individual and group) Performance appraisals Cost-benefit analyses

PLANNING FOR SYSTEMATIC PROGRAM EVALUATION

There is no one acceptable way for conducting a program evaluation (Brandenburg, 1982). Rather, a number of models or descriptions of the process have been developed (Chalofsky, 1985; Federal Highway Administration, 1977; Gane, 1972; Kirkpatrick, 1976; Knowles, 1980; Laird, 1985; Nadler, 1982). A composite description of how to design a systematic evaluation process, using ideas from the various authors cited, is given in Table 12.2. The process contains nine steps. For each step, operational guidelines with a specific on-the-job example are outlined.

TABLE 12.2. A Nine-Step Process for Planning and Conducting a Systematic Program Evaluation

Steps	Operational Guidelines	Example
1. Identify the individuals to be involved in planning and overseeing the evaluation	An individual or team of individuals should be designated to plan and oversee the program evaluation process. Some larger organizations have personnel designated for this function. Others choose to hire outside consultants.	Two staff members from the training department are responsible for the overall design and conducting of the evaluation. They will consult with other staff (e.g., managers, supervisors, trainees) as needed.
2. Define precisely the purpose of the evaluation and how the results will be used.	The purpose of the evaluation should be clearly stated and understood by all parties involved. It is especially important to meet the expectations of top management and the supervisors of those being trained in defining the purpose.	The major purpose of this evaluation is to determine whether the training program has produced a major change in the job performances of trainees. A secondary purpose includes the improvement of the training program itself.
3. Specify what will be judged and formulate the evaluation questions.	Five major areas can be judged: (1) Participants' learning; (2) Participants' job performances; (3) Impact on the organization; (4) Impact on training unit's policies, procedures, practices, etc. The specific questions should address the purpose of the evaluation.	The major item to be judged is the participants' change in job performances with the secondary item being the training program itself. The evaluation questions are: (1) Was there a change in the job performances of the participants as a result of the training program? (2) Was this change in job performances maintained over a nine-month period? (3) How could the training program be changed to better meet the changing job needs of the trainees?

193

TABLE 12.2. A Nine-Step Process for Planning and Conducting a Systematic Program Evaluation *(continued)*

Steps	Operational Guidelines	Example
4. Determine who will supply the needed evidence.	Evidence can be gathered from participants, their supervisors, training staff members, instructors, mangement personnel, and outside consultants.	Primarily, evidence will be gathered from participants and their immediate supervisors. Training staff will also be asked to supply some of the materials.
5. Specify the evaluation design to be used.	Choose a design that matches the evaluation purpose, questions, and nature of the program. Examples of quantitative evaluation designs include one group pretest and posttest, one-group time series, and one nonrandomized control group. A qualitative design could also be used. The optimal choice of design may not always be the most feasible or practical.	A one-group time series design is chosen to measure the change in the job performances of participants. A qualitative format will be used to examine the training program itself.
6. Determine the data collection techniques to be used.	The techniques chosen should be based primarily on the purpose of evaluation and design chosen. In addition, the characteristics of the respondents, the expertise of the evaluators, and the time and cost requirements should be considered.	Three primary techniques will be used to conduct the evaluation: interviews, written questionnaires, and a review of performance records.
7. Specify the analysis procedures to be used.	The analysis procedures are related directly to the evaluation questions, design, and kind of data collection techniques used. For quantitative data, they can range from simple numerical counting or percentage reporting to very sophisticated statistical analysis. Qualitative data is usually reported in prose form, though some simple numerical tables are also used.	As the quantitative data are at nominal level, the analysis will consist of frequency counting and a chi-square statistical procedure. The qualitative data will be analyzed using a content analysis procedure.

TABLE 12.2. A Nine-Step Process for Planning and Conducting a Systematic Program Evaluation *(continued)*

Steps	Operational Guidelines	Example
8. Specify what criteria will be used to make judgments about the program.	The criteria chosen indicate the level of performance or change that will be considered acceptable. Criteria should be set for each major evaluation question.	Sample criteria based on the quantitative data are: (1) The participant must demonstrate he or she can make X% more widgets within an eight-hour shift after the training program than; before; and (2) The participants will make X% less reject products after the training program than before. For qualitative data the criteria are less clear-cut. Rather, a judgment is made based on trends and themes that emerge from the data.
9. Determine the time frame and the budget needed to conduct the evaluation.	The time frame may be a set time (e.g., before and after a specified program) or be done on a continuous basis (e.g., recording of change in the learning of participants for all training programs). Program evaluations cost money, so a realistic budget should be negotiated prior to initiating the process.	The time-frame for the quantitative evaluation is: Pretest 1: April Pretest 2: June Pretest 3: August Treatment: September Posttest 1: October Posttest 2: March Qualitative data will be collected throughout the project. The budget for the evaluation has been set at $10,000.

DESIGN OPTIONS FOR SYSTEMATIC PROGRAM EVALUATION

There are two approaches used for program evaluation: quantitative and qualitative. The quantitative approach involves numerical measurement, while the qualitative focuses more on verbal or written "thick" descriptions. A single approach can be used or the two approaches can be combined. These approaches yield very different types of data as shown in the examples given in Table 12.3 (Boyle, 1981).

There are a number of standard designs within the quantitative approach. Four of these designs are described in Table 12.4 (Brethower and Rummler, 1979; Chalofsky, 1985; Cook and Campbell, 1979; Kerlinger, 1986).

195

TABLE 12.3. Examples of Different Types of Data Produced by Quantitative and Qualitative Evaluation Approaches

Focus of Evaluation	Quantitative Approach	Qualitative Approach
Participants' learning	Changes in test scores of trainees that measure knowledge, skill levels, and/or attitudes.	Opinions by the instructor on the extent of change in trainees' knowledge, skill levels, and/or attitudes.
Participants' job performances	Direct on-the-job observations and recordings by the trainees' supervisors, using a behavioral checklist, of specific job behaviors stressed in the training session.	Trainees describe in open-ended interviews how they believe their job performances have changed.
Organizational policies, procedures, practices, and functions	Changes in the absentee rate of the trainees noted over a six-month period.	Opinions from the trainees' supervisors that the trainees appear to have changed their job performances (e.g., appear more motivated).
Training unit's policies, procedures, practices, and functions	Trainees rate, using a five-point Likert Scale, a specific aspect of a training program (e.g., content, instructors, and the instructional techniques).	Training staff recall how well a training program was conducted and the extent to which they believe the program was successful.

Although some authors (Laird, 1985; Smith and Delahaye, 1983) stress using the control group design, this is usually not practical for evaluating most training programs. It is difficult, due to time and budget constraints, to set up in the work setting a control group, especially a randomized one. For example, many times the training program was needed yesterday and thus the time and effort is not available to conduct a control group design evaluation.

The other three quantitative designs (one-group posttest, one-group pretest/posttest, and time series) are not as scientifically rigorous as the control group design, yet in the workplace they usually are more acceptable and doable. Each design has its drawbacks, but also can be useful depending on the objectives of the evaluation (Chalofsky, 1985; Cook and Campbell, 1979). The one-group posttest provides a snapshot of the trainees' knowledge, skills, or attitudes after training. This information may be useful for descriptive purposes or in making decisions about future offerings. But no statements can be made about the effectiveness of the program in terms of changes in the participants' performances or knowledge.

TABLE 12.4. Examples of Standard Quantitative Designs

Type of Design	Description	Timing of Design
One-group posttest-only design ("one-shot case study")	Evaluating a single group only once after that group has completed a training program. Data are gathered in a posttest procedure.	Give training → Posttest
One-group pretest/posttest design	Collecting data both prior to the training and after the training on one group of participants. This allows for comparison of the individual's or group's knowledge level, skill, or attitude change.	Pretest → Give training → Posttest
Time-series design	Multiple observations/testing over time of a group of trainees. The observations/testing may be on the same group of trainees or can be made on a second, but similar group. The expected outcome is that the knowledge, skills, or attitudes would be different after the training.	Pretest 1 → Pretest 2 → Pretest 3 → Give training → Posttest 4 → Posttest 5 → Posttest 6
Control group design	A comparison between two groups. Both groups are given a pretest. Then one group is given the training, followed by a posttest. The control group may be chosen randomly (an experimental or randomized experiment) or be a separate, intact group that has comparable characteristics (nonequivalent group design).	Pretest both groups → Divide into two groups → [Experimental group → Give training → Posttest] / [Control group → No training regular work → Posttest]

The one-group pretest/posttest design allows for contrasting what trainees knew, felt, or how they performed before training and what they knew, felt, or how they performed after training. The major difficulty with this design is "its failure to ensure that the training or treatment, is the only factor causing the pretest/posttest differences" (Chalofsky, 1985, p. 1469). A second drawback is that giving a pretest to trainees may influence the way they respond to the posttest.

The time-series design also permits training personnel to compare the knowledge, skills, and/or attitudes of the trainees prior to and after training. Measures are taken a number of times after the training is completed and those changes that are the most enduring can be highlighted. As with the one-group pretest/posttest design, the major disadvantage with this design is being unable to state with certainty that the training program, not other influences (e.g., change in personnel, salary increases), caused the trainees to change.

The qualitative approach to evaluation provides in-depth descriptions, usually in the form of words and/or pictures rather than numbers (Bogdan and Biklen, 1982; Patton, 1981). The data are primarily gathered through individual and group interviews, observations, videotaping, and/or reviewing documents and records. The data are usually analyzed by content analysis, with the emphasis on finding ideas or themes that appear throughout the information sources. The written results of the analysis, the themes that were discovered, "contain quotations from the data to illustrate and substantiate the presentation" (Bogdan and Biklen, 1982, p. 28). This evaluation design is especially appropriate in evaluating the training programs on "soft skills" (e.g., interpersonal skills, building self-confidence) for which exact outcomes are difficult to quantify.

TECHNIQUES FOR COLLECTING EVALUATION DATA

There are a number of techniques that can be used to collect evaluation data. A technique can be used alone or in concert with one or more techniques, depending on the purpose and design of the evaluation and the type of information needed. In addition, the types of people administering and responding to the evaluation and the cost of using the technique are also important variables to consider. Seven of the most widely used techniques for collecting evaluation data are displayed in Table 12.5. A description is given of each technique, along with a list of operational guidelines and evaluation approaches for which the technique is appropriate (Chalofsky, 1985; Federal Highway Administration, 1977; Knowles, 1980; Spencer, 1985; Steadman, 1980; Tracey, 1984).

TABLE 12.5. Techniques for Collecting Evaluation Data

Technique	Description	Operational Guidelines	Appropriate Evaluation Approaches
Observations	Watching trainees while they work at actual or simulated job tasks and recording the knowledge, skills, and/or attitudes that trainees display.	Can be open-ended or structured with specific variables to investigate. Observers must have a clear picture of what they should be observing, who, and how.	Quantitative and qualitative
Interviews	Conversations with people (e.g., trainees, training staff) individually or in groups, either in person or by phone.	Can be open-ended or formally structured with specific questions to ask. For formally structured interviews, pretest interview questions. Interviewer must listen and not judge responses.	Quantitative and qualitative
Written questionnaires	Gathering of opinions, attitudes, perceptions, or facts by means of a written series of questions.	Can use a variety of question formats: open-ended, ranking, checklists, scales, and forced choices. Can be administered through mail or given to individuals or groups to complete.	Primarily quantitative
Tests	Consists of paper and pencil, or performance tests. Used to measure a trainee's knowledge, skills, or attitudes.	Know what the test measures (knowledge, skills, or attitudes) and use as an evaluation tool only for those areas. Check to see that the test is both reliable and valid. Choose a test carefully. Check to see if what it measures is important and relevant.	Primarily quantitative
Trainee products	Products that trainees produced for review (e.g., rebuilt engine, set of written reports, audiovisual presentation, repaired equipment).	The products wanted should be clearly and precisely defined. The trainee, if possible, should be able to use the product on the job.	Quantitative and qualitative

TABLE 12.5. Techniques for Collecting Evaluation Data (continued)

Technique	Description	Operational Guidelines	Appropriate Evaluation Approaches
Organizational records and documents	Written materials developed by the organization. Examples include: performance appraisal reports, production schedules and reports, audit reports, records of absenteeism, job efficiency indexes, and annual reports.	Data should be systematically collected and recorded so that it is easy to retrieve.	Primarily quantitative, although some of the written materials may be of a qualitative nature
Cost-benefit analysis	A method for assessing the relationship between the outcomes of a training program and the costs required to produce them.	Develop the cost side of the equation. Include both direct and indirect costs. Calculate the benefits side by focusing either on increasing revenues or decreasing expenses. Must have quantitatively measurable outcomes to use this technique.	Quantitative

Many of the same techniques are used both for program evaluation and needs assessment. This overlap is not surprising as often pretest data are acquired through needs analysis. For example, information gathered by on-the-job observations as part of a needs analysis could be used as baseline data for an evaluation study. After the training program was completed the change in job performance would be measured against that original needs analysis data. The type and form of the data would need to be equivalent in both phases.

ALTERNATIVE WAYS TO EVALUATE TRAINING PROGRAMS

Although most models of program development advocate a formal or systematic program evaluation, informal evaluations of programs and their outcomes can also be helpful (Federal Highway Administration, 1977), as illustrated in the following three examples:

EXAMPLE ONE. John C., the Assistant Director of Nursing, has been developing a three-session staff development program for all management-level nurses in the hospital. At various points in the planning process he has talked with a number of the staff asking their opinions on various aspects of the program, from the format and content to what he should serve for food and drink at the coffee break. Two of his colleagues have been especially helpful in helping him choose the instructors and types of instructional methods to use.

EXAMPLE TWO. The atmosphere of the workshop was tense. The morning presenters had not delivered what they had promised and the participants were very verbal about how poor the program had been thus far. Sally R., the Program Coordinator, decides to call an emergency meeting over lunch with all of the workshop staff. Prior to the meeting she spends a quick 15 minutes with two of the participants, getting their reactions to the morning session. Armed with that information and her own perceptions, Sally decides to "lay the major problems on the table" and hopes that the presenters will be able to respond in a positive and useful way.

EXAMPLE THREE. Christina A., the Vice President for Human Resource Development, decides to attend part of the new training programs for the nonexempt personnel. She is interested in finding how receptive the employees are to the training events. Christina randomly chooses three sessions to attend when the time they are being offered fits into her schedule. She times her arrival and departure around the coffee break so she can hear what the trainees are saying informally about the program.

When training personnel evaluate informally, they may not even be aware they are doing an evaluative process. Often these informal evaluation sessions are done over lunch or coffee. Staff talk about the merits of the program and its overall strengths and weaknesses. In addition, they may address specific aspects of the program, such as the planning process itself, the content, or the effectiveness of the instructors.

KEEPING USEFUL TRAINING RECORDS

Good training evaluations depend on useful and usable information. Therefore, it is important to keep accurate training records. These records should be as lean and uncomplicated as possible (Flynn, 1985). Only needed information should be collected and stored.

There is a variety of information that may be helpful to record for later use in evaluating training programs. This includes four broad categories of data, as shown in Table 12.6.

TABLE 12.6. Categories of Information for Training Records

Categories of Information	Example
Baseline data on trainees' performance prior to training	Information is collected on the performance of trainees by their supervisors prior to the start of training. In addition, the instructor administers a written test at the beginning of the training program.
Evaluation data on trainees after individual instructional units	Information is collected on the performance of trainees by their supervisors at the end of the training program. In addition, the instructor administers a written test at the end of the last training session.
Evaluation data on trainees' performance after completing a training program	Information is collected on the performance of the trainees by their supervisors six months after the training program has been completed.
Evaluation data on the training itself	Information is collected from the program participants and the instructors on each individual session and on the program as a whole.

The information recorded should be directly related to the goals and objectives of the program and the organization as a whole. The data should serve as background material when demonstrating that specific program and perhaps overall organizational objectives have been achieved.

Flynn (1985) has suggested four guidelines for keeping useful training records:

1. One person should be responsible for collecting and entering data and for monitoring the training records.
2. Data should be entered on a systematic and continuous basis.
3. Data should be collected and recorded so that it can easily be retrieved.
4. Where possible, both individual and group training records should be kept.

In summary, the key terms usability and usefulness should guide the process of recording and storing information for evaluating training programs.

SUMMARY

1. Program evaluation is the process used to determine the effectiveness of the training activities and the results of those activities. The heart of program evaluation is judging the value or worth of a training program.

2. The program objectives serve as the basis for program evaluation. The purpose, design, and criteria should be drawn from these objectives.

3. Results of the program evaluation can demonstrate that changes in the participants or the organization have actually occurred, and if not, why not.

4. Participant evaluation is the most generally used form of evaluation. Another common evaluation indicator is reporting: (1) the number of participants, (2) the number of hours in the program, and (3) the number of sessions and topics covered.

5. There is no one acceptable way for conducting a program evaluation. One nine-step process for planning and doing evaluations is:

    1. Identify the individuals to be involved in planning and overseeing the evaluation.

    2. Define precisely the purpose of the evaluation and how the results will be used.

    3. Specify what will be judged and formulate the evaluation questions.

    4. Determine who will supply the needed evidence.

    5. Specify the evaluation design to be used.

    6. Determine the data collection techniques to be used.

    7. Specify the analysis procedures.

    8. Specify what criteria will be used to make judgments about the program.

    9. Determine the time frame and the budget needed to conduct the evaluation.

6. There are two approaches used for program evaluation: quantitative and qualitative. The quantitative approach involves numerical measurement, while the qualitative focuses more on verbal or written "thick" descriptions.

7. Seven of the most widely used techniques for collecting evaluation data are:

> Observations
> Interviews
> Written questionnaires
> Tests
> Trainee products
> Organizational records and documents
> Cost-benefit analysis

A technique can be used alone or in concert with one or more techniques, depending on the purpose and design of the evaluation, and the type of information needed.

8. Although most models of program development advocate a formal or systematic program evaluation, informal evaluations of programs can also be helpful. Often these informal evaluations are done over lunch or coffee.

9. Good training evaluations depend on useful and usable information. Therefore, it is important to keep accurate training records. These records should be as lean and uncomplicated as possible.

10. Four categories of information should be recorded and stored:
    a. Baseline data on trainees' performance prior to training
    b. Evaluation data on training after individual instructional units
    c. Evaluation data on trainees' performance after completing a training program
    d. Evaluation data on the training program itself

1. Briefly describe a training program for which you need to do a systematic evaluation.

_____

_____

_____

_____

2. Using the following nine-step process, develop a plan for evaluating the program you described in item 1.

Steps	Your Evaluation Plan
1. Identify the individuals to be involved in planning and organizing the evaluation process.	
2. Define precisely the purpose of the evaluation and how the results will be used.	
3. Specify what will be judged and formulate the evaluation questions.	
4. Determine who will supply the needed evidence.	

(continued)

Steps	Your Evaluation Plan
5. Specify the evaluation design to be used.	
6. Determine the data collection techniques to be used.	
7. Specify the analysis procedures to be used.	
8. Specify what criteria will be used to make judgments about the program.	
9. Determine the time frame and the budget needed to conduct the evaluation.	

► CHAPTER 12, WORKSHEET 2:
ALTERNATIVE WAYS TO EVALUATE TRAINING PROGRAMS

List at least three ways, other than a systematic evaluation process, that you have used in evaluating training programs. Indicate next to each alternative whether what you did was helpful, and describe briefly why or why not.

Alternative Ways for Evaluating Training Programs	Was this way helpful? Briefly explain why or why not.
1. _____ _____ _____ _____	_____ _____ _____ _____
2. _____ _____ _____	_____ _____ _____
3. _____ _____ _____	_____ _____ _____

► CHAPTER 12, WORKSHEET 3: KEEPING USEFUL TRAINING RECORDS

1. List two training programs for which you need to keep records.

   Training Program 1: _____

   Training Program 2: _____

2. Using the following chart, outline how you would collect the information and indicate whether you would keep individual and/or group records. You may not wish to use all four categories of data.

Categories of Information	Program 1		Program 2	
	Data Collection Technique	Kind of Data Needed (Individual and/or Group)	Data Collection Technique	Kind of Data Needed (Individual and/or Group)
Baseline data on trainees' performances prior to training				
Evaluation data on trainees after individual instructional unit				
Evaluation data on trainees' performances after completing a training program.				
Evaluation data on the training program itself.				

13

CARRYING OUT THE PROGRAM

Bill Q. is busily checking on all the last minute program arrangements for a three-day conference that starts tomorrow. The conference is being held in one of the local hotels. This is the first time he has used these facilities so he has been double-checking all the arrangements, such as accommodations, food, and equipment. Bill plans to go over to the hotel later in the day to again meet with the hotel sales director to make sure all is in order. Bill's major worry at this point is the weather. Rain with heavy fog is forecasted and this could wreak havoc with the arrival of both conference participants and speakers. He has been thinking all day about possible contingency plans if one or more of the major speakers is not able to arrive on time. Bill has called an emergency meeting of the conference planning committee to help him work out the details of a possible reorganization of at least day one of the conference. This committee will meet later over dinner.

Most personnel who coordinate training programs agree that the actual carrying out of the program can be a very hectic and busy time. All of the program arrangements must be checked and thought must be given to how the program should be opened, monitored, and closed. One person may be responsible for all these tasks, including the instructional portion of the program, or a number of people may be involved, depending on the complexity of the training event.

Smith and Delahaye have stressed how visible the coordination function is. "Although often unaware of many of the fundamental aspects of the training function, trainees are immediately affected by the details of coordination and form judgments based on their impressions of those details" (Smith and Delahaye, 1983, p. 271). Thus it is important that training programs be well-coordinated, with special attention paid to details that directly affect the participants.

OVERSEEING THE PROGRAM ARRANGEMENTS

One of the first tasks of the program coordinator is to ensure all program arrangements have been completed. This should mostly be done the day before, although some aspects of the arrangements, such as checking on room set-ups, may only be done on the day of the program. A program arrangements checklist, listing the items that need to be finalized prior to the start of the program (Davis and McCallon, 1974; Munson, 1984; Nadler 1982; Smith and Delahaye, 1983) is given in Table 13.1.

TABLE 13.1. Program Arrangements Checklist

Items To Be Checked	Points To Be Considered Related to Each Item
Facilities to be used for training (e.g., training rooms break-out rooms)	Lighting
	Ventilation
	Temperature
	Lay-out of room (e.g., arrangement of table and chairs, placement of equipment)
Meals and breaks	Menus reflect what was requested
	Final count of people for each meal and break time
	Exact times for meals and breaks
Sleeping accommodations	Reservations in order for both participants and staff
	Rooms are clean and comfortable
Instructors and program	Training staff have a clear understanding of their roles
	All presenters, leaders, instructors accounted for
Equipment	Type requested
	Number of each type of equipment needed
	Working properly
	Backup supplies (e.g., bulbs)
Materials	Completeness of items
	Number of copies
	Arranged in order of use
Travel	Type
	Who is responsible
	When transportation is needed and for whom
Program schedule	Pace and timing
	Ways to keep on schedule
On-site registration	Procedures
	Physical set-up
	Times site will be open

The key to finalizing the program arrangements is that everything should be in place prior to the arrival of the participants (Munson, 1984). There is nothing more frustrating to trainees than having a training event appear disorganized before it even begins.

OPENING THE PROGRAM

It is crucial at the opening of any training event to create a positive climate for learning. Knowles has spoken often to this point, "I am convinced that what happens in the first hour or so of any learning activity (course, seminar, workshop, institute, tutorial, etc.) largely determines how productive the remaining hours will be" (1980, p. 224).

Climate setting starts as soon as the participants arrive. Are the participants greeted warmly and perhaps given a cup of hot coffee, or are they allowed to just wander in and find a spot for themselves? Is there someone available to introduce the participants to one another and provide name tags? Are the people responsible for on-site registration friendly and helpful or do they seem to just be doing a job? Do they growl at participants who have problems with their registration materials or do they really try to be of assistance? Does the coordinating staff seem harried or do they appear calm and in control?

The way participants are oriented at the beginning of the program is also important (Knowles, 1980). Introduction of staff and participants should be made first (Knowles, 1980; Knox, 1986). The training personnel are usually introduced to the training group as a whole. If there are numerous staff members only introductions of key personnel, such as the program coordinator and the primary instructors and resource people, should be made at this time. All these introductions should be short and sweet.

If the group is small (12 or less members), then the introductions of the participants should be done in one group. If the number is greater than 12, the group should be divided into small groups. Although this does not allow the learners to get to know all the other participants, it does give them the opportunity to become better acquainted with some of them. This type of activity is especially important when the learners do not know each other at all or just have a "passing acquaintance." Knowles (1980) has outlined four items participants could share with each other as a way of introducing themselves:

1. Present and past work roles and training experiences
2. Characteristics about themselves that make them unique as individuals (e.g., hobbies, interests)
3. Special resources they bring to the training event (e.g., previous training and experience)
4. Special problems, issues, or questions they are hoping to get assistance with through the training activity

It is also important, as a result of the orientation procedure, that learners should have a clear understanding of: (1) the objectives of the program, (2) the program requirements (e.g., attendance, participation, outside learning assignments), and (3) the expectations the instructors have for participants and the participants' expectations for instructors (Nadler, 1982). This orientation can be done formally through a short presentation or it can be completed more informally, such as reviewing the above items in small groups. The more informal style may help the participants get better acquainted and give a greater opportunity for learners to ask more in-depth questions about the training event.

At this time, it is also helpful to spell out any additional ground rules for the training activity (Davis and McCallon, 1974). For example, the participants may wish to know how and when they can receive messages. Laird (1985) has pointed out that some messages are urgent, others are not.

Critical personal messages usually involve a family crisis and should be delivered immediately. Critical work-related messages can be defined in two ways: (1) the trainee is needed back on the job and thus must leave the training session, or (2) information from the trainee is necessary for work back on the job to progress, thus the trainee must call his or her office on the next break (Laird, 1985). Critical work-related messages should also be delivered to the participants immediately after receiving them or during the next break. All less urgent messages should be left at a central spot for participants to pick up at the end of the day.

OPERATING AND MONITORING THE PROGRAM

Nadler (1982) has emphasized that things will and do go wrong during training sessions. Some of these things may be out of the coordinator's control, like a principle speaker being sick. Other problems may have been avoidable, such as having insufficient copies of training materials or nonfunctioning equipment. No matter what the source of the problem, the key is to find a solution that will allow the program to keep functioning at an optimal level. This means the program coordinator must remain flexible and be highly creative at times. For example, if a principal speaker is ill, perhaps a second speaker could be found or the order and timing of the program rearranged. This calls for some fast action on the part of the coordinator and the ability to make sound, but quick decisions.

Even if the program appears to be running smoothly, it is important that the program coordinator makes sure this is so. This includes checking to see that: (1) all resource people are there and prepared, (2) rooms continue to be arranged as requested, (3) equipment is available and working, (4) food and refreshments are delivered on time and are well prepared, (5) correct training materials are available, (6) appropriate evaluation data are being collected as planned, and (7) the schedule is being followed by the presenters (Davis and McCallon, 1974; Smith and Delahaye, 1983).

An additional way to monitor the program is to have the participants give feedback to the program staff at designated times during the training event. This type of feedback is especially useful for programs of more than one day, when changes in the program's format or content could realistically be made. There are a number of ways this could be accomplished, from administering short written questionnaires to having the respondents critique the program in small groups.

One intriguing way of doing this via small groups is to conduct focus group interviews with selected participants (Long and Marts, 1981). Semistructured questions are used to find out what the participants think of the programs. The participants' perceptions are then fed back to the program staff so changes can be made in the program for the next day. These groups should be integrated into the program and not just tacked on at the end of each session or day. Trainees should be selected at random to participate and be given an invitation that requests their involvement. A sample invitation is given in Table 13.2.

The job of discussion leader when using the focus group is critical. The leader should be well versed in the process and be willing to record and feed back all comments, no matter how negative.

TABLE 13.2. A Sample Invitation to a Group Evaluation Interview

Your feelings about today's program are important to us. But rather than ask you to fill out another questionnaire, we invite you, instead, to meet for a few moments with a small group of other conference goers _____ at _____
in _____ .   (date)   (time)
    (room)

There you'll have an opportunity to describe what, for you, were the highs and lows of today's program.

The information from each small group will be recorded and reviewed with conference planners to design appropriate follow-up.

We hope the discussion proves worthwhile to you, too. We want you to come. If you're not able to take part today, then you're welcome to trade dates with someone or just come when you can.

Thanks!

Name(s) of evaluator(s)

SOURCE: Long, James S. and Julia A. Marts. *The Focused Group Interview—An Alternative Way to Collect Information to Evaluate Conferences.* Pullman, Washington State University, 1981, Attachment A. Reprinted with permission.

The program is being monitored, whether by staff and/or participants, and it is important that the feedback is used to make program adjustments. These adjustments could range from making sure the time schedule is followed to altering the content of the program. It is the responsibility of the program coordinator to ensure the necessary changes have been made.

TIPS FOR PROGRAM INSTRUCTORS

"The behavior of the instructor is without a doubt the single most potent force in establishing a climate" for learning (Knowles, 1980, pp. 225-226). Instructors can enhance learning by being willing to share their content mastery, by using appropriate teaching techniques, and by establishing good rapport with the training participants (Knox, 1986; Stark, 1985).

It is vital that instructors know their material and have a clear understanding of the backgrounds and experiences of trainees. Instructors can obtain information about the participants from registration forms, through the introduction process, and by listening closely to what they have to say throughout the training event (Munson, 1984).

Motivating participants up front is a very important part of the instructors' responsibilities (Munson, 1984). One major way to capture trainees' interest is to get them personally involved with the material. This could be done by starting with a question-and-answer period or breaking the group into small work teams. However participation is fostered, it should be well planned and applicable to the program content. There is nothing worse than starting a training program in an unorganized and vague manner. A second way to motivate the group is by having enthusiastic and energetic instructors. Being open to questions and comments, using humor, and interacting in an active manner can spark the interest of even the more reluctant participants.

In assisting trainees to learn content, it is necessary that the material be presented in an organized and logical manner. As outlined in Chapter 11, a number of different instructional techniques can be used, with the emphasis placed on trainee participation whenever possible. Some "helpful hints" for instructors are given in Table 13.3 (Knox, 1986; Michalak and Yager, 1979; Munson, 1984).

It is important that instructors assist the participants in examining how the skills, new knowledge, or attitudes they have learned can be applied on the job. This can be done in two primary ways: (1) by using applications exercises (e.g., role playing, return demonstrations, simulations), and (2) by having trainees develop an individual plan for how they will use their newly acquired knowledge, skills, and/or attitudes.

TABLE 13.3. Helpful Hints for Instructors of Training Sessions

Remove or lessen anxieties of the trainees.

Use language that all participants can readily understand and avoid jargon words.

Communicate material in small bites.

Break up complex ideas into smaller and simpler ones.

Give participants signals (e.g., five reasons) to help them follow the ideas presented.

Maintain eye contact with participants.

Vary the speed at which you speak.

Make sure everyone in the room can hear both the instructor and the participants.

Talk from notes, rather than from a formally prepared script.

Restate important ideas.

Be generous with examples.

Listen carefully to all ideas presented by the participants and respond appropriately.

Keep a good pace.

Provide positive reinforcement to participants throughout the session.

Give practice time.

When participants develop an individual plan or contract, a draft of this should be prepared during the training time. Trainees should then negotiate final copies of their plans with their immediate supervisors. A sample form for doing an applications learning plan is pictured in Table 13.4.

TABLE 13.4. Individual Plan for Application of Training on the Job

List Knowledge, Skills, and/or Attitudes Learned	Outline How This Could Be Used on Your Job	Specify How You Will Know that You Are Successfully Using the New Knowledge, Skills, and/or Attitudes	Provide a Target Date for You and Your Supervisor to Review Your Progress
_____	_____	_____	_____
_____	_____	_____	_____
_____	_____	_____	_____
_____	_____	_____	_____
_____	_____	_____	_____
_____	_____	_____	_____
_____	_____	_____	_____

CLOSING THE PROGRAM

In closing the program, two tasks need to be accomplished. The first is to ensure that all data needed for the evaluation have been collected. Depending on how the evaluation was designed, the data collection could have been completed throughout the training and/or at the end of the program. Whenever the process is done, it is helpful to have some kind of incentive for trainees to give the needed information. For example, a candy bar or a piece of fruit to eat on the way home could be given to participants after completing their participant reaction forms at the end of a program.

Second, it is important to give trainees recognition for participating in the program (Nadler, 1982). One common practice for doing this is to award certificates to all trainees who have successfully completed a program. "If a formal certificate is inappropriate, some other written document may still be used. It could be a letter from a high-level company official or other written notice" (Nadler, 1982, p. 221). Some minimum requirements should be set in order for the trainees to receive the certificates or other written notification. These requirements may range from attendance to having participants demonstrate that learning has occurred.

TYING UP LOOSE ENDS

The coordinator has the responsibility for tying up all the loose ends after the program is completed. A number of tasks, such as picking up extra training materials, returning equipment, and scrutinizing the bills, need to be done. It is helpful to make a closing checklist prior to the start of the training program. That way, tiredness is less likely to overcome the need to pay attention to the wrap-up details. A sample checklist follows (Davis and McCallon, 1974; Smith and Delahaye, 1983):

Tasks To Complete After the Program

_____ Clear training rooms and put back in order

_____ Pick up and store extra training material

_____ Check out and store training equipment

_____ Complete all administrative form

_____ Scrutinize and pay all bill

_____ Conduct a staff debriefing

SUMMARY

1. Most personnel who coordinate training programs agree that the actual carrying out of the program can be a very hectic and busy time. All the program arrangements must be checked and thought must be given to how the program should be opened, monitored, and closed.

2. It is crucial at the opening of any training event to create a positive climate for learning. Climate setting starts as soon as the participants arrive.

3. As a result of the orientation procedures, participants should have a clear understanding of:
    a. The objectives of the program
    b. The program requirements
    c. The expectations the instructors have for participants
    d. Their expectations for the instructors

4. Things will and do go wrong during training programs. No matter what the source of the problem, the key is to find a solution that will allow the program to keep functioning at an optimal level. This means the program coordinator must remain flexible and be highly creative at times.

5. In making sure the program is running smoothly, the program coordinator should check to see that:
    a. All resource people are there and prepared
    b. Rooms continue to be arranged as requested
    c. Equipment is available and working
    d. Food and refreshments are delivered on time and are well prepared
    e. Adequate training materials are available
    f. Appropriate evaluation data are being collected as planned
    g. The schedule is being followed by presenters

6. Instructors are potent forces in the training environment. They can enhance learning by being willing to share their content mastery, by using appropriate teaching techniques, and by establishing good rapport with training participants.

7. Some sample helpful hints for instructors are:
    a. Use language that participants can readily understand and avoid jargon
    b. Break up complex ideas into smaller and simpler ones
    c. Maintain eye contact with participants
    d. Be generous with examples
    e. Provide positive reinforcement to participants throughout the session

8. It is important that instructors assist participants in examining how the skills, new knowledge, or attitudes they have learned can be applied back on the job. This can be done in two primary ways:
   a. By using applications exercises during the training
   b. By having trainees develop an individual learning plan for how they will use what they have learned in their work

9. Closing the program involves two tasks: (1) ensure all data needed for the evaluation have been collected; and (2) recognize the trainees for their participation in the program.

10. The coordinator has the responsibility for tying up all the loose ends after the program is completed. It is helpful to make a closing checklist prior to the start of the training program. That way tiredness is less likely to overcome the need to pay attention to the wrap-up details.

▶ CHAPTER 13, WORKSHEET 1: OVERSEEING THE PROGRAM ARRANGEMENTS

Reflect on a training program you have recently coordinated. Using the following chart, critique the program arrangements that were made. Place an "NA" (not applicable) next to those items for which program arrangements were not needed.

Categories of Items	What Was Good About the Arrangements?	What Problems Were There with the Arrangements?	How Could the Arrangements Have Been Improved?
Facilities for training			
Meals and breaks			
Sleep accomodations			
Instructors and programs			

(continued)

Categories of Items	What Was Good About the Arrangements?	What Problems Were There with the Arrangements?	How Could the Arrangements Have Been Improved?
Leaders			
Equipment			
Material			
Travel			
Program schedule			
On-site registration			

▶CHAPTER 13, WORKSHEET 2: CREATING A POSITIVE CLIMATE FOR LEARNING

1. Describe briefly a training session for which you will act as the coordinator.

   _____

   _____

   _____

   _____

2. Outline, using the following chart, how you would create a positive climate for learning.

Part of the Program	How Would You Handle Each Item To Help Create a Positive Climate for Learning?
Registration	
Introduction of staff	
Introduction of participants	
Introduction of the program	

1. Briefly describe a training program you recently attended to help improve your work. _____

_____

2. Complete an individual plan, as outlined in the following chart, for how you will apply what you learned on your job.

Individual Plan for Application of Training on the Job			
List Knowledge Skills, and/or Attitudes Learned	Outline How this Could Be Used On Your Job	Specify How You Will Know that You Are Successfully Using the New Knowledge, Skills, and/or Attitudes	Provide a Target Date for You and Your Supervisor To Review Your Progress

3. Review this plan with your immediate supervisor and make changes as appropriate, and note those changes below.

_____

_____

_____

14

MEASURING AND APPRAISING THE RESULTS OF THE PROGRAM

Too often program evaluation data are collected and then left on someone's shelf or in a computer file. If this is to be the fate of the information gathered, it is better not to collect the data at all because just gathering the data may raise unfounded expectations that the information will actually be used to make decisions about the training program.

The measurement or data analysis phase of the evaluation process involves determining, by some objective means, whether the goals and objectives of the program have been achieved. The appraisal, or data interpretation process, is the more subjective judgment of how well these program objectives have been accomplished and whether or not each objective was a worthwhile endeavor (Houle, 1972). The end product of measuring and appraising the results of the program is a judgment of the worth or value of the training program (Houle, 1972; Boyle, 1981; Federal Highway Administration, 1977).

COLLECTION OF EVALUATION DATA

Evaluation data are collected at three major points in the training process: (1) prior to training, (2) during training, and (3) after training is completed. The types of information collected at these three major points and where and how this information is gathered are outlined in Table 14.1. At whatever point the evaluation information is collected, it is important to have set procedures for both analyzing and interpreting the data.

TABLE 14.1. When, Where, What, and How Evaluation Data Are Collected

When Data Are Collected	Where Data Are Collected	Type of Data Collected	Example of How Data Are Collected
Prior to the start of the training program	On-the-job At the training site	Baseline data on trainees' present knowledge, skills attitudes, and/or job performances Baseline organizational information (e.g., present costs, absentee rate, turnover, accident rate	Pencil and paper tests Performance tests On-the-job observations and interviews Review of organizational records Questionnaires
During the training program	At the training site	Participants' learning Participants' reactions to the training program while it is still in progress	Pencil and paper tests Performance tests Questionnaires Interviews
After the training program is completed	At the training site	Participants' learning Participants' and staff's reaction to the training program	Pencil and paper tests Performance tests Questionnaires Interviews
Follow-up studies	On-the-job	Participants' job performances Organizational level information (e.g., change in absentee rate, costs, turnovers)	Pencil and paper tests On-the-job observations and interviews Review of organizational records

DATA ANALYSIS

One of the most frequent flaws in the evaluation process is the inadequate planning of the data analysis procedures (Knox, 1986). The following scenario illustrates this problem:

> Karen W., the manager of a training division for a large manufacturing company, has been asked to prepare an evaluation report covering the

last two years of the training program. She believes this should be a fairly easy process as she requires that evaluation information be collected on all programs.

Due to time constraints of her staff, very little actual analysis of the data has been completed, especially in the last year and except on new training events. Karen decides to do a cursory review of data prior to turning the information over to two of her staff who will actually complete the analysis and do a draft of the report. To her dismay, what she finds on the computer reports are a bunch of figures that do not make sense. Not only have the data been entered differently across programs, but the data recorded are not consistent from program to program. She also finds five file boxes full of written questionnaires that have never been entered into the system and a large stack of handwritten notes from evaluation interviews with key management staff. Karen wonders how she and her staff are going to make sense out of all these different sets of data.

The data analysis draws together all the data collected into a useful set of categories so judgments can be made about the program (Chalofsky, 1985; Knox, 1986). These judgments usually come in the form of conclusions and recommendations. For some program evaluations, only a single data source, such as a major questionnaire or a series of performance tests, is needed. For other evaluations, data may have to be merged from different sources so that complete responses to the evaluation questions can be provided. This concept of single and multiple data sources is illustrated in Table 14.2.

If the data analysis is not clearly outlined beforehand, it can be especially problematic when multiple data sources are used. This could be seen earlier in the scenario describing Karen W.'s dilemma.

Choosing data analysis procedures depends on the design of the evaluation and the type of data collected. For quantitative designs, some sort of numerical values are assigned, from simple counting to complex statistical analysis (Cook and Campbell, 1979; Laird, 1985). Qualitative analysis provides more in-depth descriptions, usually in the form of words or pictures rather than numbers (Bogdan and Biklen, 1982; Patton, 1981). Content analysis is one of the most often used methods for reviewing qualitative data.

If training personnel are unfamiliar with the data analysis process, especially when complex procedures are needed, it is usually a good investment to hire an outside consultant. "People with such expertise may be higher education specialists or may be engaged in evaluation or market research in a business or community agency" (Knox, 1986, p. 168).

TABLE 14.2. Sample Evaluation Questions and Data Collection Techniques for Single and Multiple Data Sources

Type of Data Source Needed	Sample Evaluation Questions	Sample Data Collection Techniques
Single data source	What new skills were learned by trainees as a result of the training program on supervisory skills?	Pretests and posttests of performances
	Was there a reduction in the rate of turnover for new employees as a result of the orientation program?	Review of company turnover rates for new employees
	Did participants feel the instructors were effective in the training program on communicative skills?	Questionnaire
Multiple data sources	What changes in the participants' job performances resulted as an outcome of the management development program?	On-the-job observations Interviews Performance appraisals
	Did the training of line supervisors in personnel skills result in a cost savings to the organization?	Review of company records Cost-benefit analysis
	Are the training personnel effective instructors and/or coordinators of training programs?	Questionnaires Observations Interviews

In reporting the evaluation findings, Nadler (1982, p. 224) stresses that

> *what is most important is that those who are expected to read the analysis should clearly understand what has happened. . . . The end result of the learning should be stated so that the reader does not have to wonder about the meaning of a particular number or table.*

Thus it is the responsibility of training personnel to review the evaluation report and make sure the audience can understand how the data analysis was completed.

INTERPRETATION OF THE DATA

Interpreting the data involves making judgments on the worth of the program based on information compiled during the analysis phase. It is bringing together various pieces of the information and supplying answers to the evaluation questions (Chalofsky, 1985). Was what the participants learned in a program worthwhile in relationship to what they actually do on the job? Were the objectives of the program completed in an effective and efficient manner? Does management personnel believe the training program is a vital resource to assist in fulfilling the goals and objectives of the organization? The judgments made during the data interpretation phase provide the basis for making the final conclusions and recommendations concerning the content and the operation of the training program.

The data should be interpreted in reference to the criteria developed to judge the success of the program. The results of the analysis are compared with the initial criteria set for each evaluation question or objective. For those criteria that are measurable, the judgments are quite simple. The changes produced by the program either meet the criteria as stated or they do not. Examples of this are given in Table 14.3.

TABLE 14.3. Examples of Evaluation Questions, the Criteria Set for Each Question, the Findings, and the Interpretations and Conclusions Made Based on Those Findings

Evaluation Question	Criteria	Findings Based on Analysis Process	Interpretations and Conclusions
Participants' Learning			
Did the participants in the program on supervisory skills gain sufficient knowledge in this content area?	Participants will score 85 or better on a knowledge test on supervisory skills.	Thirty-eight of the participants scored 85 or better on a knowledge test of supervisory skills.	The majority of trainees mastered the material and thus the program was termed highly successful.
Participants' Job Performances			
Was the change in the trainees' job performances maintained over a six-month period?	Trainees will make 6% or less reject products in an eight-hour shift two weeks after the training program. They will maintain that record for a six-month period following the training.	Eighty percent of the trainees made 6% less reject products after the training session and maintained that level for a six-month period. The remaining 20% did not meet this goal.	As a large majority of the trainees did meet the criterion, the program was labeled as useful in helping to solve the problem of producing too many reject products.

TABLE 14.3. Examples of Evaluation Questions, the Criteria Set for Each Question, the Findings, and the Interpretations and Conclusions Made Based on Those Findings (continued)

Evaluation Question	Criteria	Findings Based on Analysis Process	Interpretations and Conclusions
Organizational Policies, Procedures, Practices, and Functions			
Was there a reduction in the turnover rate for new employees as a result of the orientation program?	There will be a reduction of 25% in the turnover rate of new employees over a six-month period.	The turnover rate was reduced by 10% during a specified six-month period.	The training program did not produce the desired effect and thus the problem of high turnover rate needs to be examined for alternative solutions.
Training Unit's Policies, Procedures, Practices, and Functions			
Are the training personnel effective up-front instructors for in-house training programs?	The instructors will be rated a four or better on a five-point scale on their skills as up-front trainers. The data will be drawn from 25 randomly selected training programs over a six-month period.	All but one of the training personnel were given an overall four point average based on the data drawn from 25 program evaluations of randomly selected training programs.	The training staff as a whole were seen as very effective up-front instructors for in-house training programs.

Although it is recommended that evaluation criteria be defined in measurable terms, this is not always possible or desirable, as "the effort to be completely objective can lead to a tendency to seek only those goals whose accomplishments are readily measurable and to forget the rest" (Houle, 1972, p. 183). These judgments are more difficult to make and yet they still need to be done.

In interpreting the evaluation data on a training program, both the successes and the failures should be examined in terms of the realities of the situation (Houle, 1972). Too often only the successes are highlighted, while trying to understand the failures is neglected. Sork (1981) has outlined a systematic process, termed the postmortem audit, for analyzing program failures. This process is useful for reviewing specific training activities and not the program as a whole. Sork cautions that postmortem audits can be very difficult to do because not all the facts may be known and what are known may only be products of peoples' minds or imaginations. Eight important questions that could be used for such an audit are:

1. What was the dollar value of personnel time devoted to this activity?

2. About how much money (other than for personnel) was expended on this activity?

3. What event(s) initiated our involvement with this activity or, restated in the colloquial, 'How did we get into this mess?'

4. Why was this activity judged to be related to our goals?

5. What event or evidence led to this activity being judged a failure?

6. What are the consequences associated with this failure?

7. What could have been done to avoid this failure?

8. What should be done to avoid future failures like this?

SORK, THOMAS J. "THE POSTMORTEM AUDIT: IMPROVING PROGRAMS BY EXAMINING 'FAILURES.'" *Lifelong Learning: The Adult Years*, VOL. 5, No. 3, P. 31 (NOVEMBER 1981). REPRINTED WITH PERMISSION.

Postmortem program audits should be timely and include as many staff who were involved with the program activity as possible.

FORMULATING RECOMMENDATIONS

The final step in the evaluation process is formulating recommendations concerning the training program. The recommendations should focus on the future directions of the program. Alternative courses of action for responding to the issues raised should also be presented in the recommendations section. Recommendations can be made regarding: (1) the planning and delivery of the program, (2) the program content, (3) the program outcomes, and (4) how the training function could more effectively and efficiently serve the organization. For example, it might be recommended that supervisory personnel become more active in planning training programs for their personnel, but the recommendation should not stop there. It should also address how these supervisory personnel should become involved (Chalofsky, 1985).

A proposed format for outlining program recommendations is:

Major Conclusions	Recommended Actions	Strategies for Addressing the Recommended Actions

The conclusions should be grouped by major issues or topics and address the original evaluation questions. These are followed by clearly described recommended actions and ways these actions could be carried out.

Chalofsky (1985) states that recommendations regarding further evaluation efforts may also be helpful. These recommendations could address such issues as the usefulness of the evaluation questions, the appropriateness of the design and data collection techniques, and the clarity of the analysis and reporting procedures. For example, specific recommendations could be made concerning the format and questions on an instrument used to gather evaluation information. Perhaps the language of the questionnaire was too technical and the length too long; thus the questionnaire was cumbersome for many of the respondents to complete.

SUMMARY

1. Too often evaluation data are collected and then left on someone's shelf or computer file. If this is to be the fate of the information gathered, it is better not to collect the data at all.
2. Evaluation data are collected at three major points in the training process: (1) prior to training, (2) during training, and (3) after training is completed.
3. The data analysis draws together all the data collected into a useful set of categories so judgments can be made about the program. One of the most frequent flaws of evaluation is inadequate planning of this phase of the process.
4. Choosing data analysis procedures depends on the design of the evaluation and type of data collected. For quantitative designs, some sort of numerical values are assigned, from simple counting to complex statistical analysis. Qualitative analysis provides more in-depth descriptions, usually in the form of words or pictures.
5. Interpreting the data involves making judgments about the program and then using these judgments to answer the evaluation questions. The data should be interpreted in reference to the criteria developed to judge the success of the program.
6. In interpreting the evaluation data on a training program, both the successes and failures should be examined. A postmortem audit is very useful for analyzing program failures.

7. The final step in the evaluation process is formulating recommendations concerning the training program. The recommendations should focus on the future directions of the program and include alternative courses of actions for responding to the issues raised.

8. Recommendations can be made regarding:
   a. The planning and delivery of the training program
   b. The program content
   c. The program outcomes
   d. How the training function could more effectively and efficiently serve the organization

1. Briefly outline a training program for which you need to do a systematic evaluation.

_____

_____

_____

_____

2. Using the following chart, outline when, where, what, and how the evaluation data should be collected. Complete only those portions of the chart that are appropriate to your situation.

When Data Should Be Collected (Prior, During, and/or After Training	Where Data Should Be Collected	Type of Data To Be Collected	How the Data Should Be Collected

► CHAPTER 14, WORKSHEET 2:
ANALYZING THE EVALUATION DATA

1. Briefly ouline a training program for which you need to do a systematic evaluation.

_____

_____

_____

_____

2. Outline, using the following chart, what type of data will be collected, from what data sources, and how you will analyze that data.

Type of Data To Be Collected (Quantitative/ Qualitative or Combination)	Proposed Data Source(s)	How Data Will Be Analyzed

►CHAPTER 14, WORKSHEET 3: FORMULATING PROGRAM CONCLUSIONS AND RECOMMENDATIONS

Using information from a program evaluation you have recently completed, fill in the following chart. Are there any blank spaces? If so, how would you complete them if you had a chance to redo the same evaluation process?

Evaluation Question	Evaluation Criteria	Findings	Con-clusions	Recommen-dations	Action Strategies

15

COMMUNICATING THE VALUE OF THE PROGRAM TO THE APPROPRIATE PUBLICS

Tom G., the Vice President for Human Resource Development for a large power company, has just met with all the training directors from the various operational centers for the company. The majority of these directors had voiced concern over the lack of visibility for the training function. Although these directors felt they and their staff were doing a commendable job, their perceptions were that they received very little recognition for their work, especially from top management. They had asked for help on how to tell their story better so it would be heard by the right people. Tom wonders what kind of advice he should give to the directors and what his role should be in enhancing the image of the training operation.

Communicating the value of the training function to the appropriate publics is often overlooked (Boyle, 1981). Although training personnel do generate reports on their operations, these reports tend to be uninteresting and dull. Even when the reports are lively and interesting, no real thought may be given concerning how to get key decision-makers to review and then use the information.

PREPARING REPORTS ON TRAINING

There are five important factors to consider when preparing training reports (Boyle, 1981; Knowles, 1980; Knox, 1986): (1) function, (2) scope, (3) audience, (4) content, and (5) format.

Function of the Report

A training report may fill one or more major functions. The report can be used to assist in decision making about current and future programs, for accountability, and/or as a basis for promotion and public relations (Boyle, 1981; Knowles, 1980). The staff responsible for preparing the report must have a clear understanding of how the report will be used prior to putting it together.

Scope and Audience

Decisions must also be made about the scope and the audience for the report. The scope refers to how comprehensive the report will be. Will the report describe only a specific training event, selected part of the training operation, or the training program as a whole?

The audience includes all those who receive the report. There may be one or multiple audiences depending on the function and the scope of the communication. Common audiences for training reports include:

1. Trainees
2. Instructors
3. Training staff
4. Supervisors of trainees
5. Top management
6. Training advisory committees
7. Clientele of the organization
8. The general public.

Content

The content is the information that will be included in the report. A typical content outline for a training report is:

Content Outline for Training Report

---

1. Description and objectives of the training program or event
2. Outline of the process used to generate the report
3. Description of the results of the program or event
4. Listing of recommendations for future actions

The content should be organized around the issues and concerns of the recipients of the report (Knox, 1986).

Format

The format is how the information is to be communicated to the appropriate audience(s). This can be done in a number of ways as outlined in Table 15.1.

TABLE 15.1. Formats for Training Reports

Format	Description
Formal written report	A formal written report describing in complete detail the objectives, results, and recommendations of the program. The depth and scope of the report depends on the purpose and audience for the document.
Executive summary of formal written report	A one- or two-page summary of a formal written report, highlighting the major components of that report. This summary may be found at the beginning of the complete report and/or be distributed separately.
Journalistic style report	A report written in newspaper style describing the major results of a program. If possible, pictures should be included in a report of this nature.
Media presentation	A formal presentation using some kind of media, such as slides, videotapes, or transparencies. Often formal oral reports are enhanced by the use of audio-visual aids.
Case study report	A report that describes a specific training event, incident, or situation. The case is used to illustrate a major facet of the program.
Product display	Products produced as a result of a training program are put on display. This is usually used in combination with a second format, such as a written report or an informational brochure.
Poster or display board	A sign illustrating the results of a training program. It could be used as part of an oral presentation or placed in a strategic place in the organization where key personnel will be able to see it.
Oral report	A formal or informal oral presentation, highlighting specific aspects of a training program. Although this type of report can be planned, it is often given on a spontaneous basis at staff or committee meetings.
Informational brochure	A written document that describes the results of a specific program or series of programs. It can be mailed to key people, placed in display racks, or handed out in organizational meetings or future training sessions.

A single format may be used for one report or a combination of formats may be more effective. For example, although a formal written report with an executive summary may be developed, in presenting that report training personnel may wish to use slides and display board material to illustrate the important content of the document. Whatever format or formats are chosen, the challenge is to find the best way to present the information so that the audience will be receptive and willing to use the materials (Chalofsky, 1985).

In preparing training reports, it is helpful to map out each of the five factors prior to developing the report. A method for doing this, with specific examples given for each factor, is illustrated in Table 15.2. Completing this task should make it easier to develop a report that is well organized, clear, and concise.

COMMUNICATING THE REPORT TO KEY INDIVIDUALS AND GROUPS

"Reports should be made frequently to individuals and groups intimately involved in the program" (Knowles, 1980, p. 190) and at least annually to top management and as appropriate to the public at large. As stressed earlier in this chapter, the audience for the report should be chosen carefully prior to the report preparation. The information has a much better chance of being "heard" if it is in the language and the "mind-set" of the primary receivers.

Table 15.2. Five Important Factors To Consider when Preparing Training Reports, with Examples Given for Each

Primary Function	Scope	Audience	Content	Format
Program decision making	The technical training program	Instructors Supervisors Training staff Technical training advisory committee	Subject matter of the training program Effectiveness of instructors and program coordinators On-the-job performance changes resulting from the training program	Journalistic-style report Product display Oral reports
Program accountability	The training program as a whole	Vice president for human resource development Other top management	Cost-effectiveness of the program	Formal written report with executive summary Oral presentation with use of audio-visual materials
Program promotion and public relations	A specific training event	Potential trainees and their supervisors	Results of the training program	Informational brochure Posters placed in in high visibility areas

The timing of the report may be critical in terms of whether the information is actually used (Weiss, 1972). For example, a report sent to trainees' supervisors during their busiest production season will probably be put aside or given only a very cursory review. On the other hand, a report sent to these same supervisors during budget preparation time, which demonstrates that their production costs were reduced by 5 percent as a result of training, will in all probability be given a very thorough review. Thus, based on the practical realities of the work environment, it is important to plan not only to whom and in what format, but also when the report should be released. A sample chart for completing this task is given in Table 15.3.

In summary, when communicating the value of the training function, training personnel should make sure the reports are clear and understandable. Careful thought should be given as to the appropriate audience and the timing of the reports.

TABLE 15.3. A Sample Chart for Planning Training Reports

Report Content	Who Recieves	Format of Report	When Report Should Be Released
Technical training, a three-year review	Instructors Technical supervisors Training staff Technical training advisory committee	Journalistic-style report	Mid-June (a time when production is normally slow)
An evaluation of the management development training program	Entry- and mid-level managers Top management Training staff	Formal written report with executive summary	September 1 (one month prior to the start of the new program year for the Management Development Program)
The wellness program, a one-year report	All company personnel	Informational brochure Poster displays	January 1 (after the holiday season)

CONDUCTING FOLLOW-UP ACTIVITIES WITH KEY INDIVIDUALS AND GROUPS

Follow-up activities may be needed with key individuals and groups to clarify questions or concerns about the program or just to make sure the information has been heard. These follow-up communications can be formal, such as disseminating further written documents or conducting formal interviews; or they may be more informal, such as having conversations over coffee or lunch. For example, Walter R., the director of training, believes it is important that all department heads of the company thoroughly understand the implications and recommendations of his recent training report. Thus he and his associate director will meet personally with each of the department heads to discuss the report and respond to any questions they may have. Walter decides to send each department head, prior to their meeting, a second copy of the executive summary of the report, with an addendum outlining what action steps the training department has taken thus far. In addition, Walter plans to "buttonhole" many of the assistant department heads over coffee or lunch to gather their opinions on the report.

SUMMARY

1. Communicating the value of the training function to the appropriate publics is often overlooked.
2. Five important factors should be considered when preparing training reports: function, scope, audience, content, and format.
3. A training report may fill one or more major functions. The report can be used to assist in decision making about current and future programs, for accountability, and/or as a basis for promotion and public relations.
4. The scope of the report refers to how comprehensive the report will be. The audience includes all those who receive the report, and the content is the information that will be included in the report.
5. The report format is how the information is to be communicated to the appropriate audiences. This can be done through:
   a. Formal written reports
   b. Executive summaries of formal written reports
   c. Journalistic style reports
   d. Media presentations
   e. Case studies
   f. Product displays
   g. Poster or display boards
   h. Oral reports
   i. Informational brochures.

6. The timing of the report may be critical in terms of whether the information is actually used. Thus, based on the practical realities of the work environment, it is important to plan not only to whom and in what format, but also when the report should be released.

7. When communicating the value of the training function, training personnel should make sure the reports are clear and understandable.

8. Follow-up activities may be needed with key individuals and groups to clarify questions or concerns about the program. These follow-up communications may be formal (e.g., written documents) or informal (e.g., conversations over coffee or lunch).

▶ CHAPTER 15, WORKSHEET 1: PREPARING REPORTS ON TRAINING

1. Describe briefly a situation for which you need to prepare a report on a specific training event or program.

_____

_____

_____

_____

2. Using the following chart, outline the primary function(s), scope, audience, content, and format for that report.

Factors To Consider	Your Report
Primary Function(s) **Decision making** **Accountability** **Promotion**	
Scope **Single training event** **Series of training events** **Whole training program**	

Factors To Consider	Your Report
Audience **Trainees, instructors, training staff, supervisors, top management, advisory committee, clientele of organization, general public**	
Content **Information to be included**	
Format **Written report, journalistic style report, media presentation, case study report, product display, posters, oral report, informational brochure**	

► CHAPTER 15, WORKSHEET 2:
COMMUNICATING THE RESULTS OF THE TRAINING
PROGRAM TO KEY INDIVIDUALS AND GROUPS

Using the following chart, develop a one-year plan for communicating the results of your training program to key individuals and groups, both internal and external to the organization.

Content of the Report	Who Should Receive Information	Format Report Should Take	When Report Should Be Released or Given

16

USING THE MODEL: A CASE STUDY

A program planning model is meant to be used, not left on a shelf in someone's office. Thus, when a colleague, Rhonda Sadler, asked if she could test out and use the model in a special work assignment involving a major program development effort, this author readily accepted with pleasure.

THE SETTING FOR THE CASE STUDY

Rhonda Sadler, Training Manager, is employed by Blue Cross and Blue Shield of Virginia (BCBSVA). It is the state's oldest and largest health benefit company. In operation since 1935, the firm now covers 1.8 million Virginians statewide. Approximately 2000 employees work in 13 locations in Richmond and in 14 offices elsewhere in the state.

The company provides a full line of benefits through Blue Cross and Blue Shield programs and affiliated firms like HMO PLUS. Product lines include traditional hospital and medical coverage as well as prescription drug, dental, nursing home, and related benefits. The corporation offers literally thousands of combinations of benefits, rates, and policies—all of which are subject to change at least annually. Keeping employees well informed about this vast amount of information is a mammoth task for company trainers.

The company is in the process of implementing a new claims processing system, CHIPS (Comprehensive Health Insurance Processing System). CHIPS is a software package that replaces and integrates the current claims processing systems (e.g., Blue Cross, Blue Shield) into one operating system to provide one-step adjudication for facility and physician claims. The capabilities of the system are far-reaching and will have an enormous impact on the entire company, its provider network, and the hundreds of thousands of company subscribers.

A project team, assigned by top management, was given the task of developing and implementing the new system. One of the project subteams, managed by Rhonda, has the responsibility of designing a training program for all personnel, both internal and external to the organization, who will use the new CHIPS system.

THE PROCESS OF DESIGNING
THE TRAINING PROGRAM

One of the sources Rhonda and her staff used in the planning process was the Program Development Checklist, which was first presented in Table 4.2, and is pictured again in Table 16.1.

Rhonda found the checklist very helpful and usable. The key for her in using it was seeing the items on the checklist as separate tasks that needed to be done somewhere in the program development process, but not necessarily in the order they were listed. In fact, she found herself moving back and forth between the major activities of the checklist and completing a number of the tasks in stages, rather than all at once. This meant that many times she was working simultaneously on a number of the items. For example, using a statement of what generally needed to be done in the planning process, Rhonda first identified her staffing needs based on estimates of how much time it would take to develop each part of the training program. She then developed a budget and submitted both the staffing and budgeting documents for approval. Next Rhonda began working on defining the goals and objectives for the program, specifying the staff's responsibilities, and obtaining the needed personnel. One can see that all these tasks are on the checklist, though not necessarily at the beginning or even next to each other under the same major activity grouping. This interaction among and between components of the model is usually how the process of developing programs really happens.

TABLE 16.1. Program Development Checklist

Identify the Basis for Program Development

☐ Know the purpose of your organization, including present mission and future directions.

☐ Establish a base of support for the planning function.

☐ Spell out your philosophy of program development for adults, including your views about training, adults as learners, and the role of the trainer.

☐ Develop a formal mission statement for each training unit about the purposes and objectives of the unit.

Compile and Analyze Training Needs

☐ Conduct a formal needs assessment of present employees using a variety of techniques (e.g., task and job analyses, written questionnaires, telephone surveys).

☐ Respond to specific overall organizational needs for training (e.g., installation of microcomputers for all secretarial personnel, change in product or service, change in output levels).

☐ Use ideas generated from previous training programs.

☐ Review performance evaluation data.

☐ Respond to legislative mandates (e.g., affirmative action) and regulatory agencies (e.g., Occupational Safety and Health Administration).

☐ Review training programs from other organizations and prepackaged training programs from outside vendors.

☐ Seek suggestions from colleagues and associates.

☐ Search relevant professional literature.

Analyze the List To Determine Whether
a Formal Training Program Is Appropriate

☐ If no, determine alternative interventions.

☐ If yes, screen and prioritize the remaining items.

Prioritize Needs/Ideas/Problems for Training Programs

☐ Make explicit your assumptions underlying the planning process.

☐ Decide on personnel to do the screening and prioritizing process.

☐ Screen the needs/ideas/problems through four filters: (1) institutional purpose, (2) interests of supervisors of potential participants. (3) interests of potential participants, and (4) feasibility of the program.

☐ Prioritize the program needs/ideas that should actually be implemented and set up a master schedule for implementing these ideas.

(continued)

TABLE 16.1. Program Development Checklist (continued)

Identify Specific Program Objectives

☐ State the intended results of the program, including the expected impact on individuals (with type and number of people) and/or organizational units.

☐ Check to see that the program objectives are written in practical and concrete terms and that they will be understood by all the parties involved (e.g., participants, trainers, management).

Determine Potential Trainees, Program Format, and Staff

☐ Choose the content of the program and of the various subsections.

☐ Determine potential trainees and do a target population analysis.

☐ Choose the most appropriate program format (e.g., individualized, small or large group).

☐ Determine overall program length, times for individual sessions and subsections of the program, and potential dates.

☐ Identify staff and outline their roles (e.g., program coordinator, instructor, evaluator).

Coordinate Program Arrangements and Logistics

☐ Prepare a program budget.

☐ Obtain needed facilities and equipment.

☐ Obtain, as needed, final management approval and/or support for the program.

☐ Market the program.

Prepare Specific Instructional Plan in Cooperation with the Individual Instructor/Facilitator

☐ Define the specific role(s) of the instructors and facilitators.

☐ Define specific learning objectives for each training activity.

☐ Select and sequence content.

☐ Choose instructional techniques.

☐ Select instructional materials and aids.

☐ Develop an evaluation component for each learning activity.

☐ Prepare an instructional plan.

Formulate a Continuous Program Evaluation Component

☐ Identify the individuals to be involved in planning and overseeing the evaluation.

☐ Define precisely the purpose of the evaluation and how the results will be used.

TABLE 16.1. Program Development Checklist *(continued)*

☐ Specify what outcomes will be judged and formulate the evaluation questions.

☐ Determine who will supply the evidence you will need (e.g., participants, instructors, training staff).

☐ Specify the evaluation design.

☐ Specify what outcomes will be judged and formulate the evaluation questions.

☐ Determine who will supply the evidence you will need (e.g., participants, instructors, training staff).

☐ Specify the evaluation design.

☐ Determine what techniques you will use to collect evaluation data.

☐ Specify the analysis procedures you will be using.

☐ Specify what criteria you will use in making judgments about the program.

☐ Determine the time framework and budget needed to conduct the evaluation.

Carry Out the Program

☐ Oversee all the program arrangements (e.g., registration, equipment, rooms, meals).

☐ Create a positive climate for learning.

☐ Provide a system for monitoring the program and revise the activities as needed.

☐ Gather needed data for evaluation and record keeping.

☐ Award certificates or other appropriate recognition to the participants.

☐ Tie up all loose ends after the program is completed (e.g., store extra materials, check equipment).

Measure and Appraise the Results of the Program

☐ Analyze the evaluation data.

☐ Interpret the data and generate conclusions.

☐ Formulate program recommendations.

☐ Use this data to make decisions about new or revised training activities or alternative interventions.

Communicate the Value of the Program to Appropriate Publics

☐ Prepare a report on the program.

☐ Communicate this report to key individuals and groups.

☐ Follow up as needed with appropriate individuals and groups to clarify questions or concerns about the program.

THE END RESULT OF THE PROGRAM DEVELOPMENT PROCESS

Rhonda and her staff have completed most of the planning phases of the model. The actual implementation and evaluation of the program will come within the next year. A sample of the actual results of that planning process, illustrating the major components of the program development model, are outlined in Table 16.2.

As stressed earlier in this chapter, the development of each of the sample pieces of the CCD Training Program were not done in the order presented in Table 16.2. Rather, as the program evolved over time, the pieces of the program puzzle have been brought together to form a very complete and clear picture of the Corporate Claims Development Training Program.

TABLE 16.2. The Use of the Program Model in Planning a Training Program for Blue Cross and Blue Shield of Virginia

Identify the basis for the program development process	The Corporate Claims Development (CCD) Project is part of the overall corporate strategy of Blue Cross and Blue Shield of Virginia and is reflected in the corporation's three-year strategic plan.
	The CCD Training Program has the support of all levels of management.
	The Mission Statement of CCD Training is "to develop, conduct, and maintain a dynamic training program which meets the needs of all CHIPS users and allows for a smooth transition from the current claims systems to CHIPS." (Sadler and Lindeman, 1986, p. 3)
Compile and analyze training needs	The CCD Training Program is a response to an overall organizational need for training due to the installation of a new claims processing system. The training need is obvious as people have to learn how to use the new system to perform claims processing functions.
	A job analysis was performed for each group of users (both internal and external) to determine what knowledge they have now in relationship to what they will need to know to operate the new system.
	Additional ideas for the CCD Training Program were generated from other training programs, from existing technical training within the company, and by reviewing books and journals on such topics as change management.

TABLE 16.2. The Use of the Program Model in Planning a Training Program for Blue Cross and Blue Shield of Virginia *(continued)*

Determine priorities for training	Because the new system will change the jobs of all internal staff who interact with it, user training is a given. In addition, the provider network (hospitals and physicians) who will submit claims through the same system, also need training. Thus user and provider training were labeled top priorities. Management of the CCD Project and senior management of the corporation believe the two other areas of training—CCD Team Member Training and Promotional Training—were also important. Those who join the CCD Project will perform their jobs more proficiently after receiving the CCD Team Member Training on the overall operation of CHIPS. Promotional Training is critical to the success of the project by providing information through a variety of channels and on an ongoing basis to those who will be affected by this major corporate change.
Identify specific program objectives	The overall goals and objectives are determined for each of the four parts of the CCD Training Program: (1) CCD Team Member Training, (2) Promotional Training, (3) Provider Training, and (4) User Training. More specifically, the program objectives for the User Training Program are: (1) To develop a training program for business users designed to teach functions pertinent to file maintenance, inquiry, and claims processing, (2) To conduct CHIPS user training, (3) To develop the Initial Claims Processing Team (SWAT Team) role by gathering information from other Blue Cross/Blue Shield plans using applications similar to CHIPS, (4) To train the SWAT team, (5) To evaluate available training material by acquiring information from or attending other plans, reviewing vendor-provided documentation, and selecting BCBSVA applicable material, (6) To develop user procedure manuals by assimilating existing documentation and drafting procedures specific to BCBSVA's system (Sadler and Lindeman, 1986, p. 15). The impact, in terms of numbers and type of people who will benefit from the program, has been estimated.

(continued)

251

TABLE 16.2. The Use of The Program Model in Planning a Training Program for Blue Cross and Blue Shield of Virginia (continued)

Determine potential trainees, program format, and staff	The content of the program has been chosen and divided into four subunits: (1) CCD Team Member Training, (2) Promotional Training, (3) Provider Training, and (4) User Training.
	A target population analysis of potential trainees is planned.
	The training will be conducted in a small group format through formal classroom presentations and hands-on practice using a training version of the CHIPS system. Prior to the system training, employees will take computer-based training (CBT) courses to provide them with an overall understanding of benefits and contracts. Once employees complete CBT and classroom training, they will receive on-the-job training support from the SWAT team—the CHIPS experts.
	The overall program length, times for individual sessions, and program dates have been tentatively identified for each subprogram area. These are all recorded in a training strategy document (Sadler and Lindeman, 1986) for the CCD Program.
	The staff and their specific roles in the program have been determined. For example, the responsibilities of the staff for the User Training Program are to: (1) train the SWAT team, (2) coordinate the scheduling of User Training, (3) determine prerequisite training needed for each job function prior to beginning CHIPS training development, (4) develop and deliver user training, and (5) certify the trainees' successful completion of User Training (Sadler and Lindeman, 1986, p. 17).
Coordinate program arrangements and logistics	The program budget for the CCD Training Program was determined at the beginning of the program development process.
	The present training facilities at Blue Cross and Blue Shield of Virginia will primarily be used. In addition, some outside meeting space, depending on the audience to be trained, will be needed (e.g., for the Provider Training).

	Some additional equipment, such as personal computers, word-processing software, and mainframe computer terminals, will be obtained to use in both developing and conducting CCD Training. All other training-related equipment is currently in place (e.g., overhead projectors, white boards, slide projectors).
	The CCD Training Program and the overall CCD project will be promoted throughout the development and implementation stages in a carefully planned marketing campaign. Beginning with a regular information flow to report CCD programs to internal users, the promotion will climax with multi-media presentations to all who will be affected by the new system.
Prepare instructional plans	Curriculum development guidelines have been prepared for all training staff to use in the design of individual instructional units.
	For each course or module of instruction developed, the following will be supplied as part of a design documentation package:
	Instructional goals
	Task analysis
	Prerequisite skills, knowledge, and attitudes
	Performance objectives
	Test items
	Training plans (methodology and resources)
	Formative evaluation
	Summative evaluation
	Course revision process (Sadler and Lindeman, 1987)
	Training plans will be written using a consistent lesson plan format. Training plans will list the course objectives, time required, visual aids needed, and the methods to be used in teaching.
	"Before conducting user training, a review and approval process will be used to ensure accuracy and clarity of content" (Sadler and Lindeman, 1987).
Formulate evaluation component	Student learning, instructor skill level, and the content covered will be evaluated. In addition, the performance of the program participants will be tracked after the participants complete the training program.

| | Evaluation of student learning: By stressing a minimum of 80% accuracy in all courses, the following scale will be used to maintain this level of performance from trainees completing CHIPS training courses:
80–100: Pass
0–79: Fail
Any trainee who makes a grade of 80–100 will be considered performing at an acceptable level. Trainers will review with supervisors the performance of all trainees, with special suggestions/recommendations made for those scoring 79 or less (Sadler and Lindeman, 1987). |
| Instructor and Content Evaluation: "Each student will be given an opportunity to evaluate the effectiveness of the course content and the trainer's instructional skills on the last day of each course, using a standard evaluation form. These evaluations will be shared with the Training Manager for the purpose of identifying potential deficiencies in trainer skill, instructional design development and/or training delivery" (Sadler and Lindeman, 1987). |
	The participants' quality and quantity of performance will be traced over a period of time after completion of CHIPS training to develop a learning curve. The learning curves will then be used to assist in the development of performance standards for trainees while they are in on-the-job training.
Carry out the program	The CCD Training Program will be developed and conducted over the next two years. CCD Team Training and Promotional Training are in the process of being carried out. The design of User Training will be complete in 10 to 12 months. A User Training pilot will be conducted and content revised as needed before beginning actual User Training. It is estimated that it will take 18 months to complete the User Training.
Measure and appraise the results of the program	This process will be completed both during and after the full CCD Training Program has been completed. By developing learning curves, maintaining user completion scores, and matching both these items back to the type, length, and quality of training provided, the results of the training will ultimately be shown in the performance and productivity of employees.

TABLE 16.2. The Use of The Program Model in Planning a Training Program for Blue Cross and Blue Shield of Virginia *(continued)*

Communicate the value of the program to appropriate publics	Two major planning documents related to the CCD Training Program have already been completed. Other interim reports will be developed as needed. A final report will be written at the end of the program. The Promotional Training will maintain a high level of communication to all affected users of the CHIPS system, with anticipation that the value of training and the CCD Project as a whole will be known by users prior to and during system implementation.

SOURCES: Quotes were taken from two major documents: (1) Sadler, Rhonda and Bruce Lindeman; *Training Strategy, Corporate Claims Development*, Richmond, VA, Blue Cross and Blue Shield of Virginia, 1986 and (2) Sadler, Rhonda and Bruce Lindeman. *Training Policies, Corporate Claims Development*. Richmond, VA, Blue Cross and Blue Shield of Virginia, 1987. Reprinted with permission.

SUMMARY

1. A program planning model is meant to be used, not left on a shelf in someone's office. Rhonda Sadler, Training Manager for Blue Cross and Blue Shield of Virginia, offered to test out and use the model in the planning of a major companywide training program.
2. The "Program Development Checklist" was found to be very helpful and useful in planning the training for all personnel who would use a new claims processing system. The key to using it was seeing the items on the checklist as separate tasks that needed to be done somewhere in the program development process, but not necessarily in the order they were listed.
3. A sample of the actual results of the program planning process at Blue Cross and Blue Shield of Virginia, illustrates the major components of the program development model.

REFERENCES

Beatty, Paulette T. The Concept of Need: Proposal for a Working Definition. *Journal of the Community Development Society, 12* (2), 39–46 (1981).

Bogdan, Robert C., and Sari Knopp Biklen. *Qualitative Research for Education: An Introduction to Theory and Methods.* Boston: Allyn and Bacon, 1982.

Boyle, Patrick G. *Planning Better Programs.* New York: McGraw-Hill, 1981.

Brandenburg, Dale C. Training Evaluation: What's the Current Status? *Training and Development Journal, 36* (8), 14–19 (August 1982).

Brethower, Karen S., and Geary A. Rummler. Evaluating Training. *Training and Development Journal, 33* (5), 14–22 (May 1979).

Broad, Mary. Identification of Management Actions to Support Utilization of Training on the Job. Unpublished doctoral dissertation, George Washington University, 1980.

Caffarella, Rosemary S. A Checklist for Planning Successful Training Programs. *Training and Development Journal, 39* (3), 81–83 (March 1985).

Caffarella, Rosemary S. Identifying Client Needs. *Journal of Extension, 20* (7), 5–11 (July/August 1982).

Chalofsky, Neil E. External Evaluation. In William R. Tracey (Ed.), *Human Resources Management and Development Handbook.* New York: AMACOM, 1985, pp. 1467–1485.

Cook, Thomas D., and Donald T. Campbell. *Quasi-Experimentation Design and Analysis Issues for Field Setting.* Chicago: Rand McNally College Publishing, 1979.

Cross, Patricia A. *Adults As Learners.* San Francisco: Jossey-Bass, 1981.

Davis, Larry N., and Earl McCallon. *Planning, Conducting, Evaluating Workshops.* Austin, TX: Learning Concepts, 1974.

REFERENCES

Employee Training in America. *Training and Development Journal, 40* (7), 34–37 (July 1986).

Farlow, Helen. *Publicizing and Promoting Programs.* New York: McGraw-Hill, 1979.

Federal Highway Administration (DOT). Training Guide for Identifying, Meeting, and Evaluating Training Needs. Washington, DC: National Highway Institute, January 1977. (ERIC Document ED 143 846).

Finkel, Coleman. Pick A Place, But Not Any Place. *Training and Development Journal, 40* (2), 51–53 (February 1986).

Finkel, Coleman. Where Learning Happens. *Training and Development Journal, 38* (4), 32–36, (April 1984).

Flynn, Edward B., Jr. Internal Evaluation. In William R. Tracey (Ed.), *Human Resources Management and Development Handbook.* New York: AMACOM, 1985, pp. 1447–1466.

Forest, Laverene, and Shelia Mulcahy. *First Things First: A Handbook of Priority Setting in Education.* Madison: Division of Program and Staff Development, University of Wisconsin, Extension, 1976.

Forest, Laverene, and Shelia Mulcahy. *First Things First Workbook.* Madison: Division of Program and Staff Development, University of Wisconsin, Extension, 1976.

Gane, Christopher. *Managing the Training Function.* London: George Allen and Unwin, 1972.

Giegold, William C., and Crosby R. Grindle. *In Training: A Practical Guide to Management Development.* Belmont, CA: Lifetime Learning Publisher, 1983.

Hays, Richard D. To Market, To Market. *Training and Development Journal, 38* (6), 61–62 (June 1984).

Houle, Cyril O. *The Design of Education.* San Francisco: Jossey-Bass, 1972.

Houle, Cyril O. *The Effective Board.* New York: Association Press, 1960.

Johnson, Richard B. Organization and Management of Training. In Robert L. Craig (Ed.), *The Training and Development Handbook,* 2nd ed. New York: McGraw-Hill, 1976, pp. 2-6–2-11.

Kaufman, Roger, and Bruce Stone. *Planning for Organization Success.* New York: Wiley, 1983.

Kemp, Jerrold E. *Instructional Design,* 2nd ed. Belmont, CA: Fearon Pittman, 1977.

Kerlinger, Fred N. *Foundations of Behavioral Research,* 3rd ed. New York: Holt, Rinehart and Winston, 1986.

Kidd, J. Robbie. *How Adults Learn.* New York: Association Press, 1973.

Kirkpatrick, Donald L. Evaluation of Training. In Robert L. Craig (Ed.), *Training and Development Handbook,* 2nd ed. New York: McGraw-Hill, 1976, p. 18-1–18-27.

Knowles, Malcolm S. *The Modern Practice of Adult Education.* New York: Cambridge, 1980.

Knox, Alan. *Helping Adults Learn.* San Francisco: Jossey-Bass, 1986.

Laird, Dugan. *Approaches to Training and Development,* 2nd ed. Reading, MA: Addison-Wesley, 1985.

Lauffer, Armand. *Doing Continuing Education and Staff Development.* New York: McGraw-Hill, 1978.

Long, Huey B. *Adult Learning, Research and Practice.* New York: Cambridge, 1983.

Long, James S., and Julia A. Marts. The Focused Group Interview—An Alternative Way to Collect Information to Evaluate Conferences. Pullman: Cooperative Extension Service, Washington State University, 1981.

Mager, Robert F. *Preparing Instructional Objectives,* 2nd ed. Belmont, CA: David S. Lake, 1984.

Mehrens, William A., and Irvin J. Lehmann. *Measurement and Evaluation,* 2nd ed. New York: Holt, Rinehart and Winston, 1978.

Michalak, Donald F., and Edwin G. Yager. *Making the Training Process Work.* New York: Harper & Row, 1979.

Moore, Michael L., and Philip Dutton. Training Needs Analysis: Review and Critique. *Academy of Management Review, 3* (3), 532–545 (July 1978).

Munson, Lawrence S. *How to Conduct Training Seminars.* New York: McGraw-Hill, 1984.

Nadler, Leonard L. *Designing Training Programs: The Critical Events Model.* Reading, MA: Addison-Wesley, 1982.

Nadler, Leonard L. *The Handbook of Human Resource Development.* New York: Wiley, 1985.

Newstrom, John W., and John M. Lilyquist. Selecting Needs Analysis Methods. *Training and Development Journal, 33,* (10) 52–56 (October 1979).

Patton, Michael Q. *Qualitative Evaluation Methods.* Beverly Hills, CA: Sage, 1981.

Pennington, Floyd, and Joseph Green. Comparative Analysis of Program Development Processes in Six Professions. *Adult Education, 27* (1), 13–23 (1976).

Robinson, Russell D. *An Introduction to Helping Adults Learn and Change.* Milwaukee, WI: Omnibooks, 1979.

Sadler, Rhonda, and Bruce Lindeman. *Training Strategy, Corporate Claims Development.* Richmond, VA: Blue Cross and Blue Shield of Virginia, 1986.

Sadler, Rhonda, and Bruce Lindeman. *Training Policies, Corporate Claims Development.* Richmond, VA: Blue Cross and Blue Shield of Virginia, 1987.

Salinger, Ruth D., and Basil S. Deming. Practical Strategies for Evaluating Training. *Training and Development Journal, 36* (8), 20–29 (August 1982).

Schall, Larryette M., and James F. Douglass. Developing Training Systems. In William R. Tracey (Ed.), *Human Resources Management and Development Handbook.* New York: AMACOM, 1985, pp. 1365–1371.

Scissons, Edward H. A Typology of Needs Assessment in Adult Education. *Adult Education, 33* (1) 20–28 (Fall 1982).

Shipp, Travis. Building A Better Mousetrap in Adult Education. *Lifelong Learning, The Adult Years, 5* (1), 4–6 (September 1981).

Smith, Barry J., and Brian L. Delahaye. *How to Be an Effective Trainer.* New York: Wiley, 1983.

Smith, Robert M. *Learning How to Learn.* Chicago: Follett, 1982.

Sork, Thomas J., and John H. Buskey. A Description and Evaluation Analysis of Program Planning Literature, 1950–1983. *Adult Education Quarterly, 36* (2), 86–96 (Winter 1986).

REFERENCES

Sork, Thomas J. *Development and Validation of a Normative Process Model for Determining Priority of Need in Community Adult Education.* Adult Education Research Conference, 1979. (ERIC Document ED 169 389).

Sork, Thomas J. Determining Priorities. Vancouver: British Columbia Ministry of Education, 1982.

Sork, Thomas J. The Postmortem Audit: Improving Programs by Examining 'Failures.' *Lifelong Learning: The Adult Years, 5* (3) 6–7, and 31, (November 1981).

Spencer, Lyle M., Jr. Calculating Costs and Benefits. In William R. Tracey (Ed.), *Human Resources Management and Development.* New York, AMACOM, 1985, pp. 1486–1510.

Stark, Alexander T. Conducting Training Programs. In William R. Tracey (Ed.), *Human Resources Management and Development.* New York, AMACOM, 1985, pp. 1413–1424.

Steadman, Stephen V. Learning to Select a Needs Assessment Strategy. *Training and Development Journal, 34* (1), 56–61 (January 1980).

Strother, George B., and John P. Klus. *Administration of Continuing Education.* Belmont, CA: Wadsworth, 1982.

Tough, Allen. *Intentional Changes.* Chicago: Follett, 1982.

Tough, Allen. *The Adult's Learning Projects,* 2nd ed. Ontario: Ontario Institute for Studies in Education, 1979.

Tracey, William R. *Designing Training and Development Systems,* rev. ed. New York: AMACOM, 1984.

Tyler, Ralph W. *Basic Principles of Curriculum and Instruction.* Chicago: University of Chicago Press, 1949.

U.S. Civil Service Commission. *A Training Cost Model.* Washington, DC: Bureau of Training, Training Management Division (CST 100–0001), 1972.

Vogt, Elinore. Applying the Principles of Adult Learning. In Sam Cordes (Ed.), *Key Elements in Designing Educational Programs for Health Agency Boards.* University Park: Penn State University Press, 1982, pp. 9–13.

Warren, Malcolm W. *Training for Results.* Reading, MA: Addison-Wesley, 1979.

Weiss, Carol H. *Evaluation Research.* Englewood Cliffs, NJ: Prentice-Hall, 1972.

Witkin, Ruth Bell. *Assessing Needs in Educational and Social Problems.* San Francisco: Jossey Bass, 1984.

Zemke, Ron, and Thomas Kramlinger. *Figuring Things Out.* Reading, MA: Addison-Wesley, 1982.

INDEX